NETWORK MARKETING

First published in 2021.

ISBN: 978-1-86922-907-8 (Printed)
eISBN: 978-1-86922-908-5 (PDF ebook)

Published by KR Publishing
P O Box 3954
Randburg
2125
Republic of South Africa

Tel: (011) 706-6009
Fax: (011) 706-1127
E-mail: orders@knowres.co.za
Website: www.kr.co.za

Typesetting, layout and design: Cia Joubert, cia@knowres.co.za
Cover design: Marlene De Lorme, marlene@knowres.co.za
Editing and Proofreading: Valda Strauss, valda@global.co.za
Project management: Cia Joubert, cia@knowres.co.za

NETWORK MARKETING

Make Millions While You Sleep

Pearl Maphoshe

kr publishing

2021

Table of Contents

About the Author

Pearl Maphoshe is a Senior Human Resources Executive, Board and Corporate Governance Leader, Corporate Executive, Leadership Coach, Conference Speaker and Guest Lecturer with 29 years' experience working in Executive roles delivering business and human resources solution for JSE listed companies in the pharmaceutical, agri-processing, wholesale & retail, mining, health, education, financial services, and telecommunication industries.

She studied at the University of Durban, graduating with an Honors Degree in Economics and a Post Graduate Diploma in Education. She pursued Programmes in Educational Policy and Planning and Driving Performance through Talent Management at Harvard University to name a few. She holds a Master's Degree from the University of London. Pearl reached the peak of her career in 2018 when she was named The Best HR Director by the Institute of People Management.

She was the Group Human Capital Executive at Aspen Pharmacare Holdings. Key previous roles have included being Group HR Executive at Tongaat Hulett and Pick n Pay, Vice President HR – Africa at South 32 and Group Human Capital Executive at Massmart Group.

Pearl have been a board member at Cambridge, Masscash, University of Zululand and Wholesale and Retail SETA. She was the Chairperson of the wholesale and Retail SETA board for four years. As a Council member at the University of Zululand she also chaired the Remuneration Sub-committee of Council, and have served on the advisory boards of GIBS and the University of Johannesburg.

She currently offers specialist pedigree in the areas of Organisational Design and Effectiveness, Change Management, Leadership Development, Stakeholder Management, Employee Relations, Diversity and Inclusion, Business Partnering, Corporate Governance, Project Management, Performance Management, Talent Management, Capacity Building, Risk Management, and Strategy Development and Execution.

Introduction

My journey in network marketing started in 2001. At that time, I had the backing of a Masters degree from London University and a post-graduate qualification from Harvard University. I was already an executive and I was already enjoying all the perks of such a position. One of the things I liked about network marketing is the flexibility that is inherent in the business model. So, I signed up to run my business part-time. I did not know a lot about the network marketing industry at that stage. However, I knew the importance of diversifying my income sources. Network marketing is not an established discipline in SA universities or even in schools. There is a need to document and teach people about this lucrative business model. I have 19 years' experience in the industry and I have enjoyed success in my business. It is my intention to close the knowledge gap that exists currently on what network marketing is and how you can work it to create wealth and change your fortunes for yourself and your family now and for generations to come.

The 40-40 time-for-money trap is not for everyone. In fact, working 40 hours a week for 40 years for a salary is what I call modern-day slavery. Let me sound a warning upfront: It is a proven fact that most people will never be wealthy working a 9 to 5 job. Working a 9 to 5 locks you into a situation where you live pay-cheque to pay-cheque. Covid-19 and all other events that led to economic meltdowns serve to prove that there is no security in a job, even a high-paying one. We all work hard to achieve two main objectives i.e. **Financial Independence and Time Freedom**. We all want to be independently wealthy. We all want to get to a point where we have a stream of cash flow that keeps coming irrespective of how we spend our time. We all want to attain financial freedom so we can retire early – and start working on things that really create meaning and value for us and people around us. We want to get to a point where we do not work for money but our money works for us. Very few people achieve this noble goal. We are all looking for stability, reliable multiple sources of income and less stress. Most people work hard to achieve their dream life, but they struggle hard from pay-cheque to pay-cheque.

It is important for all of us to have multiple streams of income. A wise man once said: "You must dig your well before you are thirsty." When you have already been retrenched or when you realise at 60 or 65 that your 40-40 hustle has not helped you to create wealth, you are left not only disappointed, but you are left in a financial dark hole that will require a miracle to resolve.

Our education system does not prepare us to be opportunity seekers. It only prepares us to be job seekers. The entire education system is geared towards producing great employees who will only ever enjoy a linear income. Our education produces employees and self-employed professionals. There is nothing wrong with either of these forms generating income, except that neither form of income-generation avenues will ever give you leveraged income. To be wealthy we must cross over to entrepreneurship. Correctly set up, an entrepreneurship venture will create wealth for you through residual or even passive residual income. Warren Buffett once said: "If you have not learned how to make money while you sleep, you will work for the rest of your life." Being independently wealthy means having enough passive residual income such that you are not dependent on a job for income. This is what is called "walk away money". The fastest, most dependable and controllable way to become wealthy is to own a business. This means owning productive assets that produce cash flow. Entrepreneurship is one of the ways of creating wealth in every economy.

Entrepreneurship is important as it can improve one's standard of living and creates wealth, not only for the entrepreneurs, but also for related businesses. Entrepreneurship boosts national incomes and tax revenues. Even though entrepreneurship is the simplest way to create wealth, it comes with its own challenges:

- Lack of capital.

- Difficulties in getting loans.

- Poor knowledge of how to run a business.

- Poor access to markets.

- High failure rate.

Most entrepreneurs fail because their businesses are invisible to the world because they cannot afford to spend money on marketing and advertising. Lack of skills is another reason why most entrepreneurs fail.

The main goal of this book is to reveal a route to entrepreneurship that has created more millionaires in the history of the world compared to other industries and business opportunities. That industry is **network marketing**. Leading financial expert Robert Kiyosaki calls network marketing the business of the 21st Century. Billionaire investor Warren Buffett calls it the best investment he has ever made. *Fortune* magazine calls network marketing the best kept secret in business. Network marketing is said to be the fastest growing industry in the world. This is the industry that has freed more people from all walks of life from financial shackles. It allows entrepreneurs to imagine the retirement they desire, and it provides a proven path for them to work towards achieving that dream retirement. This is an industry that has built-in-pay-equity structure. This industry has allowed more women to achieve six-figure monthly earnings. Network marketing is the form of entrepreneurship that has the least challenges and the lowest barriers to entry and low risk compared to traditional businesses. It is accessible to everyone irrespective of financial resources, race, or educational background. Art Jonak says, "network marketing is no longer on trial. It is a proven profession that helps millions of people get ahead financially and moves many closer to their dreams." Network marketing allows ordinary people to own their businesses, work when they want, work with people they want to work with, earn income from their own effort and the efforts of the people in their team, get out of debt, work less and earn more. Jim Collins, author of *Good to Great*, says, "This business offers the most systematic way for ordinary individuals to achieve economic success." Network marketing companies have created and continue to create opportunities for people to make extra money and build wealth in a sustainable fashion. Network marketing presents everyone with an equal opportunity regardless of race, gender, educational qualification or religion, a chance to build a big business. This book will build a business case for network marketing by comparing it with a job, self-employment, start-up, and franchise business.

This book will also attempt to build a strong case for network marketing as a viable business opportunity. Chapter 1 will firstly cover the current landscape in South Africa. Statistics South Africa released a report that South Africa's gross domestic product (GDP) decreased by 51% in the second quarter of 2020 owing to the impact of Covid-19 lockdown restrictions since the end of March 2020. The poor economic outlook for the rest of the year is quite bleak. This poor outlook is expected to have a drastic impact on jobs and the livelihoods of many South Africans. Chapter 2 will cover the limitations of the traditional education system and its failure to promote financial education that will drive entrepreneurship. Chapter 3 will deal with the concept of entrepreneurship as an alternative career choice. Chapter 4 covers the franchising business model and the exorbitant cost of setting up a franchise business. Chapter 5 will define and explain the concept of network marketing. Chapter 6 will deal with misconceptions about network marketing. Chapter 7 will cover governance and ethics matters in network marketing. Chapter 8 will explore winning strategies in network marketing. Chapter 9 will cover the role of coaching in network marketing. Chapter 10 will take readers through my journey in network marketing and Chapter 11 will tell us what experts say about this profitable business model.

Chapter 1

The Current Labour Market Landscape
in South Africa

"Unemployment is capitalism's way of getting you to plant a garden".
—Orson Scott Card

The labour market refers to the supply of and demand for labour, in which employees provide the supply and employers provide the demand. In a vibrant labour market, employers compete to hire the best, and the workers compete for the most satisfying jobs. In South Africa currently, more and more people are unable to find work. South Africa's unemployment rate rose to 30.1 percent in the first quarter of 2020 from 29.1 percent in the previous period and above market expectations of 29.7 percent. It was the highest jobless rate on record since quarterly data became available in 2008, as the number of unemployed people increased by 344 thousand to an all-time high of 7.1 million. Employment fell by 91 thousand to 16.38 million from 16.42 million in the prior quarter. Total employment dropped in 7 out of the 10 industries, with the largest declines recorded in the finance industry (-50 thousand), followed by community and social services (-33 thousand), agriculture (-21 thousand), transport (-17 thousand), manufacturing (-15 thousand), construction (-7 thousand), and utilities

(-4 thousand). The expanded definition of unemployment, including people who have stopped looking for a work, was at 39.7 percent, up from 38.7 percent in the prior period.

The youth aged 15–24 years are the most vulnerable in the South African labour market as the unemployment rate among this age group was 55,2% in the 1st quarter of 2019. Among graduates in this age group, the unemployment rate was 31,0% during this period compared to 19,5% in the 4th quarter of 2018. The former Secretary of the United Nations, Kofi Annan, once said, "Unfortunately, very few governments think about youth unemployment when they are drawing up their national plans."

The South African Chamber of Commerce and Industry said that the country's unemployment rate could climb as high as 50% in line with Treasury's worst predictions. Treasury said that more than 2.5 million jobs could be cut because of the coronavirus pandemic, with wages and salaries expected to fall by as much as 40%.

Some South African companies decided to cut salaries to deal with the financial impact of Covid-19. Some companies have implemented pay reductions either on a case-by-case basis or across the ranks, and some executives have voluntarily chosen to take pay reductions. Mr Price announced that annual salary increases for head office associates have been delayed, while executive management and board of directors have committed to a cut in salaries and fees. Woolworths announced that senior executives had decided to forego up to 30% of their fees and salaries for 3 months until the end of June. EOH announced that its CEO and executive committee would take a 25% pay cut, and that it was proposing a 20% reduction across the board in cash salaries, except for those earning less than R250 000 per annum. Sappi announced that their board of directors and the group and regional leadership teams have agreed to a 10% reduction in salaries or fees for the 3 months ending June 2020. Further, the Sappi leadership teams will receive no short-term incentive bonuses for the 2020 financial year.

The above shows that as the Covid-19 outbreak continues to spread across the country, the implications of the way businesses operates will be extreme for jobs and employment. Companies have already started to optimise their workforces from the perspective of cost and the changing business environment. Companies are considering automation, free agents, and contingent workers to accomplish jobs linking workforce performance with evolving business needs.

Inadequate education and lack of productivity is costing jobs. Unemployment increases progressively with decreased educational levels and the education system is not producing the skills for the labour market. Labour supply is affected by the increase in the number of job seekers over the years.

Several South African companies are retrenching employees because of the economic meltdown and the financial crisis that the country is going through. Standard Bank, Absa and other large corporates are among those that plan job cuts. According to the CCMA's 2018-2019 financial report, in that whole year only 38 588 workers were the subjects of section 189a retrenchments. In less than three months between 1 April and 25 June 2020, 98 818 workers were the subjects of section 189a retrenchments – an increase of 156%. Workers in the retail sector could be hardest hit by the section 189a retrenchments, with 23 261 jobs at stake. Earlier in June, South Africa's biggest clothing retailer, Edcon, issued a retrenchment notice affecting at least 22 000 workers. Massmart will cut almost 1 500 jobs. Cell C plans to retrench 40% of staff. SABC plans to retrench 600 employees. Naspers plans to lay off more than 500 employees and close several newspapers and magazines. More than 14 747 private transport workers could also lose their jobs, and the hotel industry, battered by the lockdown, could see 10 387 jobs lost. These are just a few examples of the proposed retrenchments.

The impact of Covid-19 will be long lasting in the labour market. Beyond the shocking statistics of high unemployment, the nature of jobs is also changing. The economic shock from the pandemic and the lockdown will cause a reconfiguration in the labour market and redesigning of the organisational structures and the skills and competencies that are going to be valuable going forward. The workplace of the future will look quite different from the pre-pandemic era.

People are disillusion by the potential of a job as a source of income generation and as a wealth-creation vehicle. As a result, more and more people who get retrenched see **entrepreneurship** as an alternative source of income generation and a wealth-creation vehicle.

Chapter 2

The Focus of Traditional Education

"Going to school doesn't make you financially smart."
—Robert Kiyosaki

From an early age we are told to go to schools so we can get "better" jobs. Whilst this is true to a certain extent it can also be very limiting. Our education system is still geared towards careers that generate a linear income. Entrepreneurship is not taught in schools and very few universities offer entrepreneurship in their curriculum. So, in the main, traditional education channels students to be good employees and job seekers for life. Most people end up getting tied into the life of working for bosses. They get extremely disappointed at the age of 65 when they realise that even the pension they have slaved for is not enough to give them a comfortable life during their retirement. Most people struggle financially because they fail to learn 3 financial lessons that are not taught in traditional education:

- **Leverage Income**: This the ability to do more with less. Leveraged income is where you do the work once and you get paid repeatedly for doing the work. Robert Kiyosaki says, all successful people have one thing in common, and that is **Leverage.** He says that leverage is the power to earn more and more while working less and less, either by having people, or money work for you. For example, when a singer records a song once, they get paid every time the song is purchased. There are many ways of creating leveraged income. Here are a few examples: owning intellectual property, building a traditional business, network marketing and investing. In all these examples work will be done once, and you will get paid a recurring income for doing the work.

- **How to create residual/passive Income**: This is when you continue to get paid after the work is done. The key element of passive/residual income is leverage. You must be able to leverage other people's time or other people's money to create residual income. Some types of passive residual income include rental income from investment properties, investments, and savings as well as network marketing. This is where you make your money work for you. Running your own business is the tried and tested way to make your money work for you. There are two core asset classes that make people predictably rich:

  - Owning companies: a **network marketing business**.

  - Owning real estate: rental properties, commercial offices properties.

- **Linear Income**: This is income that is generated by working. In this form of income, you earn a 100% of your income from your own effort. You work once and you get paid once. This form of income is generated through being an employee, being a board member or being self-employed and is paid immediately. Examples of earned income include – working a job, consulting, speaking and any other activity that is based on time/effort spent. This is where people exchange/trade their time for money. This income-generation avenue comes with extreme risks. For instance, there is no time freedom and this type of income can lag inflation. Employees can be retrenched or fired and hence the assurance of this type of income is not guaranteed.

Traditional education only channels people toward a linear income-generation avenue through promoting jobs and self-employment. The difference between leveraged income and passive residual and linear income could mean the difference between being wealthy vs struggling and being independent or needing financial assistance.

Advantages and Disadvantages of a Job

Advantages

- You are guaranteed a pay-check at the end of the month for as long as you are employed.

- Possible to earn more, after time spent with the profession or company.

- Possible in some jobs to get benefits such as insurance or even shares.

- Possible to have paid time off and expected to work no more than 40 hours a week.

Disadvantages

- You can be fired or retrenched.

- You only make money if the company survives.

- A job is not willable.

- The 40/40 trap: Working for 40 hours per week for 40 years takes away the value of time that you could have been used in to build your residual income through network marketing.

- Your salary increase could lag inflation.

- Your salary is determined by your boss. The concept of pay-for-performance does not exist in most companies. There is so much subjectivity when it comes to salary determination.

- You must wait for someone to either be fired, quit, or die to have a chance of moving up.

- You are part of a pyramid scheme, where those on top of the company are making money, while you are at the bottom getting the scraps irrespective of how excellently you perform. Your job grade determines your station in life in a job. You get paid the same as a person you does not work as hard as you do.

- Most people earn just enough to get by until the next pay-cheque.

- You may be relocated to live where the company sees fit.

- You may be exposed to racial and gender discrimination and bullying.

The Women's Heart Foundation says the most common time for a heart attack is Monday morning. Today's stressful working environment is taking its toll on work-life balance and families.

Comparison of a Job with Network Marketing

"The richest people in the world look for and build networks. Everyone else looks for work."
—Robert Kiyosaki

Network marketing is a good career option for people with an entrepreneurial spirit. As with any business, network marketing will require a significant investment of time and effort. Done correctly, this business model is a great way to build wealth. However, there is no room for people who think they can make a quick buck with network marketing.

Advantages of network marketing over holding a job

In network marketing you can:

- Move to the top of a company if you achieve better results or work harder.

- Earn as much as you wish to if you work and earn it. Your income potential is unlimited. In network marketing distributors or network marketing entrepreneurs or independent contractors earn income – commissions and bonuses – through a **compensation plan** based on their abilities and results.

  - Work when you please and take off whenever you want. You own your time.

  - Have no boss, and work when, where, and how you wish.

  - Live a better life, not just from pay-cheque to pay-cheque.

  - Be rewarded with overseas vacations.

  - Retire at an early age and continue to enjoy passive residual income. You can retire early with more money compared to a job where you will retire late with less money.

  - Enjoy residual income (getting paid over and over for what you did years ago). This gives you time freedom and you can concentrate on other ventures.

  - Earn leveraged income from the efforts of your team.

  - Network marketing is one of the few places where women of all races earn Rand for Rand what their male counterparts earn. Network marketing offers an equal opportunity, irrespective of gender, race, educational background, or religion.

In network marketing your recognition and rewards are not based on gender, race or educational qualification. Pay for performance is the only criterion that counts in network marketing. Most importantly a network marketing business is willable. You can build a legacy for yourself and your family through network marketing.

Network marketing is the best profession to create residual income: income that continues to be generated after the initial effort has been expended. Warren Buffett once said that if you do not find a way to make money while you sleep, you will work until you die. Network marketing has a very lucrative feature that is called **Autoship**. This is a method by which shipment of products or services to a consumer is done based on a standing order supported by any form of automatic payment, e.g. debit order, for transaction purposes. It is through **Autoship** that a network marketing distributor can secure his or her commission level by meeting qualifying criteria during each earnings period.

Disadvantages of network marketing vs a job

Let us examine the downside of network marketing in comparison to a job:

- Temporary loss of social esteem. You must hear negative people say stupid things they do not understand about your choice of business.

- You realise that you should have begun sooner.

- Unlike in a job situation, there is no place to hide for underperformers in network marketing. You are paid according to the results you produce.

Self-Employment

*"Being your own boss is great; you get to choose
which 18 hours a day you get to work."*
—Unknown

Concept of self-employment defined

A self-employed person is an independent contractor or sole proprietor who reports self-employment income. Self-employed persons work for themselves at a variety of trades, professions, and occupations rather than working for an employer. This is a route that is taken by professionals such as chartered accountants, doctors, lawyers, and other tradespeople.

Self-employment is the state of working for oneself rather than an employer. A self-employed individual does not work for a specific employer who pays them a consistent salary or wages. Self-employed individuals, or independent contractors or consultants, earn income by contracting or consulting with a business directly. Self-employed people generally have several clients that they serve. Self-employed people may choose to create employment for other people should their contracts and assignments grow to a point where their individual capacity is stretched.

People get into self-employment for the following reasons:

- Good income.
- Being you own boss.
- Developing your own ideas.
- Establishing job security.

Self-employment: traits and attitudes

People who succeed in self-employment have the following characteristics:

- Able to see solutions where others only see problems.
- Educated and enjoy learning.
- Driven and competitive.
- Determined and refuse to give up.
- Willing to take a smart risk.
- Self-starters.
- Healthy and ready for long hours.
- Not afraid of failing.

Advantages of self-employment

1. Savings on some expenses: Some business expenses may be tax deductible.
2. Flexible work schedule: Self-employed people can set their own working hours. You are your own boss.
3. The end of the rush-hour phenomenon that comes with 9 – 5 jobs.
4. Freedom to choose your assignment and to choose who you work with.
5. More opportunities to earn money. This will increase your earning potential.
6. Improved quality of life.
7. Autonomy: Control over all business aspects.
8. Full use of your skills.

9. Job security: Self-employed people own their self-employment practices. Hence, they cannot be fired or retrenched.

Disadvantages of self-employment

1. Unstable income.

2. Difficulty of getting contracts.

3. Isolation.

4. Loss of a client.

5. No more paid leave and other corporate perks.

6. Multiskilling all the time: You are a generalist. You are now fully responsible for every facet of your business.

7. Self-funded benefits such as retirement and medical aid.

8. Paying taxes – as a self-employed person, you are responsible for the administration of all your tax matters.

9. No leverage: The amount of active work determines income. No work, no pay. You own a job.

Necessity for Inclusion of Entrepreneurship in the School and Tertiary Curriculum

It is high time the education system is transformed. Students should be given exposure to other forms of income-generation avenues. It is my considered view that entrepreneurship should be included in the school and tertiary curriculum. People must be shown that there are alternative revenue-generating strategies:

- Alternatives to working 40 hours a week for + 40 years as most people do.

- Alternative career options when you can work when you want, with whomever you want, and where you want.

- Career choices or business model where you to decide how much you want to earn.

In my experience that alternative career choice or business model is called **network marketing.** Network marketing is the best career/ business model that will give you residual income. Most of us only started learning about this when we embarked on a rewarding journey of self-education. Jim Rohn once said, "formal education will make you a living and self-education will make you a fortune. I can attest to that."

It is clear from the above comparison that a job or self-employment will never give you leveraged income. You will never be wealthy working as an employee. Even as a self-employed person where you own a job, you only make money from your own effort. This means that both employees and self-employed people earn what is known as linear income. To attain financial and time freedom you must own a business or productive asset that will give you leveraged income. Leveraged income is where your money is working for you. This is where you are beginning to make money while you sleep. Passive income is income that requires little or no effort to earn or maintain. This is income that you enjoy through efforts and productivity of other people in the team. In network work marketing you enjoy residual income because you do the work once and you keep getting paid long into the future. Through building a strong team you can also enjoy passive income. Network marketing gives ordinary people an opportunity to run and own their own businesses with extraordinarily little capital outlay up front.

Chapter 3

The Search for Profitable Opportunities: The concept of entrepreneurship

---

"Build your own dreams, or someone else will hire you to build theirs."
—Farrah Gray

Entrepreneurship is generally viewed as a viable revenue-generation and wealth-creation avenue. This avenue appeals to most because you get to be your own boss. There are several forms of entrepreneurship, four of which are outlined below.

Forms of Entrepreneurship

Small business entrepreneurship

Most businesses are small businesses. People interested in small business entrepreneurship are most likely to make a profit that supports their family and a modest lifestyle. These are typically businesses that employ around five people and they are always owner managed. These entrepreneurs are not seeking large-scale profits or venture capital funding. Small business entrepreneurship is often when a person owns and runs their own business. They typically hire local employees and family members. Local grocery stores, hairdressers, small boutiques, consultants, and tradesmen such as electricians and plumbers are a part of this category of entrepreneurship.

Innovative entrepreneurship

Innovative entrepreneurs are constantly coming up with new ideas and inventions. They take these ideas and turn them into business ventures. They often aim to change the way people live for the better. We find a lot of such entrepreneurs in the technology space such as software developers. Innovators tend to be very motivated and passionate people. They look for ways to make their products and services stand out from other things on the market. People like Steve Jobs and Bill Gates are examples of innovative entrepreneurs.

Hustler entrepreneurship

People who are willing to work hard and put in constant effort are considered hustler entrepreneurs. They often start small and work toward growing a bigger business with hard work rather than capital. Their aspirations are what motivates them, and they are willing to do what it takes to achieve their goals. They do not give up easily and are willing to experience challenges to get what they want. For example, someone who is a hustler is willing to cold call many people to make one sale. With the advent of technology such entrepreneurs can reach out to several people in a short space of time to demonstrate the kind of value their business could deliver to prospects. Network marketing falls into this category of entrepreneurs.

Franchisee entrepreneurship

These are entrepreneurs who buy into a franchise business. Franchisee entrepreneurs share with the franchisor knowledge of business systems. These entrepreneurs see a business opportunity and act on it – by buying a franchise business. They take a risk by buying into a franchise system although their chances of success are higher. These entrepreneurs buy into the franchise brand because they are looking for the challenge of running their own business and are ready to embrace the demands and responsibilities that that involves.

What is Entrepreneurship?

Let us define this concept of entrepreneurship now that we have outlined at least four types of entrepreneurs.

Entrepreneurship is an intentional process of an individual or a group of people, to initiate and sustain profits by production or distribution of goods or services. The International Labour Organization defines entrepreneurs as people who can see and evaluate business opportunities, together with the necessary resources to take advantage of them, and to take appropriate action to ensure success.

In simple terms an entrepreneur is an individual who actively forms or leads their own business venture and nurtures it for growth and sustainability.

Characteristics of Entrepreneurs

Entrepreneurship is an avenue that is available to everyone, but it is important to note that not everyone makes it in entrepreneurial ventures. These are some of the competencies and behaviours of phenomenally successful entrepreneurs:

- **Creativity:** Entrepreneurs enjoy inventing, experimenting, taking risks, and growing business ideas.

- **Vision:** Entrepreneurs see opportunities where ordinary people see challenges and failure.

- **Courage:** Entrepreneurs have the courage to go after their goals. They see and act on opportunities. Entrepreneurs are not easily dissuaded.

- **High energy and hard work** are the hallmarks of successful entrepreneurs: They understand that in life you get what you work for not what you wish for. Entrepreneurs are prepared to work long hours to see their dreams come true.

- **Passion and quest for excellence** drive entrepreneurs to achieve their dreams and goals.

- Great entrepreneurs have a **spirit of adventure and great imagination**.

- Successful entrepreneurs have a strong **need to achieve** and seek **personal accomplishment.**

- The high-risk nature of entrepreneurial ventures requires entrepreneurs to have a healthy dose of **self-confidence and self-belief**.

- Entrepreneurs are **persistent** and have the **attitude of winners**. They believe that they will win, maybe not immediately, but failure is not an option. Entrepreneurs are extremely tenacious. They have the bounce-back ability. They see every failure as an opportunity to do better next time.

- Entrepreneurs have a **positive attitude**. While everyone else can see risks, an entrepreneur can see the reward.

- Entrepreneurs understand that success comes from **taking initiative and following through.**

- Entrepreneurs have a **strong sense of commitment**. They understand that without commitment you will not build anything of value. It is this strong sense of commitment that builds a hard-working spirit in successful entrepreneurs.

The Benefits of Entrepreneurship

There are many reasons and benefits to starting your own business in South Africa.

Starting a business is not for everyone. People with a die-hard employee mentality do not make it in entrepreneurial ventures. Just because you can open a business, does not mean you are an entrepreneur. Starting a business in South Africa requires you to invest time, energy, and patience. But more than anything else a start-up needs passion and drive, commitment, and a clear sense of purpose. If you have what it takes and are willing to do the difficult things, then you should start your own business. After all, running your own business is the most reliable way of building wealth for yourself. Here are some benefits of starting your own business:

- Opportunity to create your own destiny and legacy.

- Autonomy – freedom to pursue your own vision. Owning a business provides an entrepreneur with the independence and flexibility to achieve what is important to them.

- Opportunity to make a difference and a sense of pride and fulfilment in accomplishing goals.

- Opportunity to reach your full potential.

- Opportunity to reap extraordinary profits.

- Social status and recognition.

- Opportunity to engage in work of your choice and choose who you want to work with.

The Downside of Entrepreneurship

Entrepreneurs face a multitude of risks, e.g. bankruptcy, financial risks, competitive risks, economic risks, poor access to markets, etc. These risks lead to the following downside of entrepreneurship:

- Uncertainty of income, low compensation and loss of corporate employee benefits.
- Requirement for high management control, e.g. labour relations matters, team management, etc.
- Challenges of acquiring finance.
- Long break-even periods.
- The risk of losing your entire investment.
- Long hours and hard work.
- Poor quality of life until the business is established.
- Extremely high stress levels.
- High failure rate of start up in SA.

Success Rate of New Ventures in SA

In South Africa, small businesses are critical to our economic development and the creation of a more equal society. With a staggering unemployment rate of over 30%, there has never been a stronger need for entrepreneurs to step up and create much-needed jobs. While entrepreneurship experts would agree with these sentiments, South Africa's small business failure rate of almost 80% within the first three years means the average entrepreneur's chance of starting a business, sustaining and growing it towards creating much-needed jobs is extremely low. Ravi Govender, Head of Small Enterprises at Standard Bank, says that although statistics vary, on average about 50% of all start-up businesses in South Africa fail within 24 months due to the inability and inexperience of their owners. Lack of finance and access to markets are also highlighted as crippling challenges by most failing entrepreneurs.

"One of the main reasons for the premature failure of small businesses in South Africa is that they are started as survivalist ventures. It is almost inevitable for them to fail because their owners do not have the skills, experience or resources to build a sustainable business," says Mr Govender of Standard Bank.

The start-up business system is touted as the incubator for innovation and a key contributor to job creation and wealth generation. It is said that most start-ups fail in their first year of operation.

Reasons to Choose A Start-Up Over a Corporate Job

A job might have a guaranteed income, salary and benefits, but it also comes with severe challenges. For as long as you work as an employee you are building someone else's fortune. You are also exposed to all the ills of the corporate world, e.g. discrimination, earnings that do not reflect what you are worth, poor leadership, etc.

Here are some of the reasons it is better to run your start-up business than to be employed:

Jim Rohn once said, "profits are better than wages". These are some of the advantages of starting up your own business over a job:

- You will have diverse responsibility.
- You will have more opportunities.
- You will be able to be innovative and exercise your creativity.
- Your work will be recognised.

- You will work in an awesome atmosphere. You will not have to deal with bad leadership from your boss.

- You will own your time.

- You will have a sense of belonging.

- You will not have to deal with discrimination and workplace bullying. Corporate politics exist in all organisations. These are activities performed by individuals to improve their status and advance their personal agenda – this is always at the expense of others. In your own start-up business, you will not have to deal with this evil phenomenon.

Overall, starting up your own business will give you a unique opportunity for growth and financial independence. Most people are not solely motivated by salary and corporate benefits. There are priceless benefits of taking the plunge and starting up your own business instead of being trapped in a job.

Chapter 4

Start-Up Costs for Franchise Businesses in SA

"If you work just for money, you'll never make it, but if you love what you're doing and you always put the customer first, success will be yours."
—Ray Kroc, Founder of McDonald's.

What is the History of Franchise?

Modern franchising came to prominence with the rise of franchise-based food service establishments. In 1932, Howard Deering Johnson established the first modern restaurant franchise based on his successful Quincy, Massachusetts, Howard Johnson's restaurant founded in the late 1920s.

What is a Franchise Business?

According to the International Franchise Association, a franchise business is a method of distributing products or services involving a franchisor, who establishes the brand's trademark or the trade name and a business system, and a franchisee, who pays a royalty and often an initial fee for the right to do business under the franchisor's name and system.

Franchising involves purchasing a unit from an already established company. When you purchase a franchise, you have access to the company's business model, business systems, advertising and marketing and products. In addition, you often receive support and training from the franchise company. In addition to the franchise purchase and set-up cost, most franchises require ongoing royalty/ franchise fees for using their brand name and business systems. Franchise opportunities exist in multiple industries, including fast food, automotive care, salon services, travel agencies and home-based cleaning services.

1. Advantages of buying a franchise business

We have explored the difficulties and the success rate of starting your own business in South Africa. Let us now explore the advantages of buying and running your own franchise business:

- Franchises offer the independence of small business ownership supported by the benefits of a big business network.

- Franchisors usually provide extensive compulsory training.

- Franchise businesses have a higher rate of success compared to start-up businesses.

- Banks are more willing to finance franchise businesses compared to innovative start-ups.

- Buying a franchise business comes with an established image, reputation and goodwill.

- Buying a franchise business comes with the established modus operandi that gives maximum support to inexperienced new business owners. This modus operandi provides tried and trusted operating procedures that guide the day-to-day running of the business.

2. Disadvantages of buying a franchise business

Let us explore the challenges and disadvantages of buying into a franchise business:

- Most franchise businesses have a cookie-cutter approach which is highly limiting, restrictive and inflexible. As a franchisee you have limited freedom within a very stringent framework. This will impact negatively on your ability to be innovative and to create your own unique business.
- Franchise set-up costs are usually extremely high.
- Buying a franchise business means ongoing sharing of profits with the franchisor.
- There are on-going franchise fees.
- The franchisor has no obligation to renew the franchise license. This means you will never really be fully independent and your ability to attain financial freedom is limited by all the financial obligations you have to the franchisee.

Some Examples of Famous Franchise Businesses in South Africa

Let us examine the famous franchise businesses in South Africa and see their requirements from entrepreneurs who are interested in owning and running them:

1. McDonald's

McDonald's South Africa estimates the cost of a franchise to be anywhere between R4 million – R6 million, depending on the type of restaurant and other factors. Applicants are also expected to have a minimum of 35% of the purchase price of a restaurant in unencumbered, non-borrowed cash.

According to McDonald's South Africa, the official cost of a franchise varies, and actual costs are only determined when an individual franchise is offered to an applicant.

2. Nando's

Nando's charges a franchise application fee of R25 000 (VAT inclusive) and a franchise fee of R230 000. This fee includes:

- The right to use and operate under the Nando's name and concept.
- Initial cover and staff training.
- Assistance with site selection and evaluation.
- Initial legal costs incurred in the conclusion of the franchise agreement.
- Assistance with lease negotiations.
- Initial pre-opening/launch assistance.

Nando's also estimates that you will need approximately R7 million (plus VAT) for establishment costs when setting up your restaurants.

3. Chicken Licken

According to the Chicken Licken website, the estimated cost of a Chicken Licken restaurant is R4.8 million. By comparison, you can expect to pay a minimum of R6.8 million for a "fly-thru" store. In both cases, you can expect to pay an initial franchise fee of R150 000. Chicken Licken also extracts a royalty fee of (6%) and advertising share (6%) that account for 12% of the franchise's turnover.

4. Roman's Pizza

The initial joining fee for a Roman's Pizza is R90,000, which the franchisors need to confirm commitment. Roman's estimates that establishment costs are approximately R2.3 million (92.17%) based on a 120 square metre store size. Costs, however, do vary in accordance with various factors and the size of the store, exchange rates, and numerous other factors that affect this estimate. Franchisees are also expected to have initial working capital of R100 000 (4.35%).

5. Steers Restaurant

Steers estimates that you can expect to pay approximately between R1.7 million – R2.5 million in set-up costs when first starting up a franchise. The company currently offers three different models with kiosk (R1.59 million), standard (R1.65 million) and drive-thru (2.35 million) options available. As with other South African franchises, there is also a franchise fee (excluding VAT) of between R114 800 and R175 700 depending on the style of franchise. Obviously, there will also be on-going profit-share arrangements.

6. Kentucky Fried Chicken

Here is the minimum requirement for KFC franchisees:

- Prospective franchisees need to show that they have the required funds to fund up to five or more stores. One store costs in the region of R6 million.

- Prospective franchisees must be prepared to undertake a training programme that can last up to 6 months. This is self-funded by the prospective franchisee and may include visiting an overseas training facility. You require a 100% pass rate to move to the next stage.

- Prospective franchisees must be able to demonstrate high business acumen (a professional tertiary education will be beneficial).

- Prospective franchisees must show leadership and demonstrate being capable of managing multi-stores.

- Prospective franchisees must be hands-on in the business and so anyone looking only for an investment opportunity will be rejected.

- Previous experience in the food industry or quick service restaurant industry is essential.

- Prospective franchisees cannot have an interest in any other food business.

- Prospective franchisees must commit 100% of their working hours to the day-to-day operation of their KFC business. (This sounds like employment to me. No time freedom).

- Prospective franchisees may have to wait for a considerable time until the right opportunity arises. They may also need to relocate.

- There is a non-refundable application fee of R5000.00 as well.

7. Sorbet

The Sorbet franchise cost starts from R1 million. According to the beauty store's latest franchising costs, you can buy a 60 square metre nail bar for around R1 million, while a Sorbet salon and Candi franchise will cost you slightly more with a total cash requirement of between R1.6 million to R1.7 million.

8. Debonair's

According to Debonair's, new franchise owners can expect to pay around R2 million. According to its website, once applicants have been granted and guaranteed a franchise, Debonair's will assist with the application for finance.

Eight South African Franchises You Can Open for Less Than R1 million

The start-up costs of the above franchises are all over R 1 million. Let us see what entrepreneurs can buy for less than that:

Postnet

As a prospective business partner, you are required to have 50% unencumbered cash. The average set-up cost for a Postnet store is R615 000 ex VAT. The setup cost will vary depending upon the store's square metreage, fixtures and fittings, landlord's contribution and equipment that is placed in the store.

Wilcote

A prospective franchisee can expect to pay R225 480 (including VAT). This initial upfront fee is payable at the commencement of training and on the date of the signing of the Franchise Agreement. Upon the opening of the franchise outlet, the amount of R294 520 (including VAT) is payable for the Plant & Equipment, Products and Office Equipment.

3@1 Business Centre

Prospective owners must prepare to part with approximately R695 000 (ex VAT).

Zebro's

The average setup cost is around R949 000 including VAT. There is also an initiation fee of R190 000 including VAT.

The Bed Shop

The up cost is averaged at R500 000 which also includes the initial franchisee fee.

Looking at all the stringent requirements and costs of opening and running a franchise business in South Africa, this business model is inaccessible to ordinary entrepreneurs that might be looking to establish a viable business. Let us quickly look at the differences between franchise business and network marketing:

COMPARISON BETWEEN FRANCHISING AND NETWORK MARKETING

FRANCHISING	NETWORK MARKETING
Seed Capital | Very High	Seed Capital | Very Low
Risk | Very High	Risk | Negligible
Break Even | 2 - 5 Years	Break Even | Immediate, Fast
Control | High	Control | Low
A lot of aspects to guard against including self discipline	The only aspect to guard against is you need self discipline

Network marketing is clearly accessible to everyone with low investment to start off with. Jim Rohn made the same observation: "Network marketing is the big wave of the future. It's taking the place of franchising, which now requires too much capital for the average person."

Challenges that Franchisees Face During Economic Downturn

During periods of economic crisis franchisees face tough financial challenges.

Shrinking disposable income

During times of economic turmoil consumers have shrinking disposable incomes and hence less money to buy luxuries. This impacts the revenues of franchise businesses. Franchisees have fixed costs that they have to deal with such as franchise fees and royalties, rent, utilities, and salaries. Franchisors can be very inflexible when change is needed.

Lack of working capital

Working capital i.e. cash flow management is critical for the successful running of a franchise business. Effectively managing a franchisee's cash flow can be the difference between just surviving and thriving in business. Working capital is essential for the day-to-day running of the franchise business but determining the amount of cash flow required to make operations run smoothly every month is not easy, especially during times of economic turmoil. Most franchisees fail because they are affected by cash flow problems. During times of financial crisis such as the Covid-19 lockdown, it becomes difficult to manage the impact of unplanned expenses such as:

1. Rising costs

Rising input costs such as electricity, fuel and other raw products is the economic reality the franchisees must deal with. These rising costs reduce the profitability of franchise businesses. It is not always possible to pass on these rising costs to consumer.

2. Rising employee disengagement and falling staff morale

Difficult operational environments such as Covid-19 lockdown and the corresponding financial implications cause additional stress for employees of franchise businesses. Further, with rising costs franchisees are not able to hire more staff or even employ people on a temporary basis. This leaves staff feeling over-stretched and demotivated. Job security issues are also heightened during this time; hence employees may fear losing their jobs. All these factors lead to a drop in employee engagement and staff morale.

3. Bad debts

The lockdown and closure of many franchise business has severely affected the cash flow of these businesses. Franchise owners may find it difficult to service their debt and borrow more money. This is bound to compromise the ability of franchise owners to expand. This will leave some franchise businesses undercapitalised.

Overall, buying a franchise means entering into a very inflexible agreement with the franchisor. Franchise agreement are very limiting. They dictate how you run the business, so there is little room for innovation and creativity. There are normally restrictions on where you operate, the products you sell, prices you charge and the suppliers you must use.

Chapter 5

What is Network Marketing?

---

*"Network Marketing is one of the simplest
paths to entrepreneurship."*

—Art Jonak

The History of Network Marketing

Network marketing has a rich history. It has created more six- and seven-figure income earners around the world. This industry has survived the 2008/2009 financial meltdown. Network is the most viable, proven and thriving business model of our modern times. Network Marketing has been around for over 50 years. In 1934 California Vitamin Company came up with a concept of network marketing. This company started out as a direct sales company signing up salespeople that would use the product for their personal use and sell to it to their family and friends.

Back in the 1930 there was a man by the name of Carl Rehnborg. Whilst in China between 1917 and 1927 he was first introduced to the benefits of using supplements in your diet and the additional health benefit that it gives people. When Carl got back to America, he set up a company called The California Vitamin Company. In 1939 he re-branded the company as Nutrilite. It was not until six years later that Carl invented the network marketing strategy to help boost the sales of his company.

The big turning point came when two new consultants, Jay Van Andel and Rich DeVos, became distributors of the Nutrilite products and noticed the real power of this business model as sales were growing at an exponential rate. They set up a competing company called Amway and bought a controlling interest in Nutrilite in 1972. In 1994 Amway then took over full ownership and is one of the leading companies in network marketing today.

What is Network Marketing?

Network marketing is also called Multi-level marketing (MLM), direct selling, or referral marketing. Network marketing is a marketing strategy for the sale of products or services where the revenue of the network marketing company is derived from a network of independent distributors that sell the company's products/services. These independent agents are rewarded through commissions, bonuses and sometimes overseas trips depending on their performance. In network marketing the concept of paying-for-performance is the basis for the very generous compensation plans.

Referral selling is the method of promoting products or services to new customers through referrals, usually by word of mouth.

Direct selling is selling products or services directly to customers in a non-retail environment. Such sales occur at home, work, online, or other non-store locations.

Network marketing is a form of direct selling. As stated, direct selling is the sale of product or service directly to customers without the need of retail infrastructure such as stores. Such sales usually take place through one-on-one presentations and similar forms of product or service exposure. Direct selling can come in single-level marketing or multi-level marketing. Multi-level marketing is a strategy some direct sales companies employ to encourage existing distributors to duplicate and recruit new distributors, not just customers. Hence the distributors will be paid commissions from their own effort and from the sales of distributors they introduce into the network.

In network marketing compensation plans pay out to network marketing entrepreneurs two **potential revenue streams**. The first income stream is paid from commissions of sales made by the network marketing entrepreneur directly to their own retail customers or first line distributors **(own effort income).** Network marketing entrepreneurs also enjoy income that is based on the efforts of distributors they introduce into the network **(leveraged income).** Building a strong team in your downline can provide multiple levels of compensation that will give you residual passive income. This leveraged income means distributors have the ability to leverage on the productivity of their teams. Paul Getty puts it aptly: "I'd rather have 1% of the effort of 100 men than 100% of my own effort."

Even with all the positives, there are many people who view network marketing in a negative light. Some of these people have tried network marketing and failed or they know someone who has failed in network marketing and so they assume that this is a bad business model. Others assume that because network marketing has a pyramidal shape it must be illegal like illegal pyramid schemes.

 Here are some of the negative things ignorant people say about network marketing:

- It is a scam.

- It is for housewives.

- It is a side business.

- It gives only some additional income that is not sustainable.

- It will fold soon.

- You have been duped.

- You will lose your money.

Why Manufacturers/Companies Choose Network Marketing as a Business Model of Choice

Manufacturers and companies use network marketing to expand their sales. Network marketing is another way of selling goods and services. Manufacturers and companies in this business model rely on several distributors to push out their products and services. The distributors build teams of sub-distributors, i.e. networks. As a result, this leads to a network of distributors that operate at various levels of the distribution chain. Hence this model is described as multi-level marketing or network marketing.

It is this business model or marketing channel that manufacturers or companies use to market their products and services directly to customers. In this model companies do not need to spend money on the expensive retail infrastructure, advertising, and marketing. The distributors act as independent representatives or agents of the manufacturer or company. This allows the company or manufacturer to save on the high costs of marketing such as advertising and salaries and benefits of a large in-house sales force.

Selling goods and services through network marketing has many advantages for companies and manufacturers.

Advantages of Network Marketing for Companies

- There are no limits on the size of the network marketing structure. There is no restriction on the number of distributors that can sign up with the company.

- The reliable and robust distribution network delivers sales to the company at a fraction of the cost. For instance, the appointment of a sales force is at a very minimal cost.

- Satisfied customers in this business model can become distributors and promote goods and services through word of mouth.

- Network marketing companies reduce the risk that is linked to employing people directly into the books. For instance, they do not have to deal with the risks of retrenching employees because distributors are not employees. In this model companies do not have to deal with strikes and disengaged employees. Network distributors are running their own independent businesses and so they cannot unionise or place unreasonable demands on the company.

- Manufacturers or companies that use network marketing to sell their products contribute positively to the reduction of the unemployment rate.

- Companies do not have to invest in huge commercial real estate to house all the distributors. This is bound to improve the profit margins for companies.

- This is an economic empowerment vehicle for companies. Through the distribution network companies can assist millions of people to create wealth and attain financial and time freedom.

- The compensation plan of the company or manufacturer is self-funding through sales. There are no fixed costs, for instance, the remuneration of distributors. The compensation plan for network marketing distributors is purely based on the number of sales made. This is not the case in terms of an in-house sales force. An in-house sales force comes with some fixed payroll cost that is not based on performance. In network marketing commissions are only paid after the distributor sells products or services. This means that cash flow is only flowing out after revenues comes in. This is a huge advantage over traditional businesses where the overhead is constant or fixed before the sale, as in payroll costs, distribution, inventory, lease agreements, etc. In the case of network marketing none of these costs are incurred.

- Low capital outlay is another advantage for companies and manufacturers that choose network marketing. Through using network marketing, companies enjoy the advantage of low cost in promoting and advertising of products and services. Network marketing companies have the capacity to scale up nationally or even internationally without having to build physical retail infrastructure.

Network marketing is good for economic advancement in general. This business model promotes skills development, entrepreneurship, and economic empowerment. Specially, network marketing helps to empower women and to close the gender pay gap that persists in most countries.

Disadvantages of Network Marketing for Companies

- Since companies or manufacturers depend on a network of distributors to determine demand, it can be difficult to predict production targets. This may compromise the company's ability to plan effectively.

- In this form of business model, the network of distributors facilitates delivery of goods and services to final customers. The companies or manufacturers have a limited role in this process. This may compromise their ability to control distribution and sales.

Why Network Marketing is the Best Business for You

Network marketing is a well-established business model that has empowered people economically and otherwise. It enables people to earn more and work less by building passive residual income sources. With network marketing you can have thousands of customers and distributors in your structure generating income for you. This is not a get-rich-quick scheme. Over time a network marketing business will lead to financial and time freedom.

Network marketing attracts overly ambitious people who are focused on success. Participants in network marketing are surrounded by a high-performance culture that supports and helps people to become successful.

What are the Benefits of Network Marketing?

• Low start-up cost

You can get started in network marketing for as little as R199 which typically includes the business fee, the cost of your product, Business App, marketing support, third-party tools, training and access to business opportunity meetings for you and your prospects. The most important requirements to start up a network marketing business are your strong desire to be successful, time commitment to work your business, and hard work. If you were considering starting up a franchise business or a traditional business, you would need at least R1 million or more. Most of these business owners do not even start to see a profit for over 3 years. Network marketing has a noticeably short break-even period. At R199 start-up cost for network marketing your break-even period is immediate.

• Leverage: The ability to earn income from the productivity of others

You can leverage yourself by having thousands of people in your organisation that pay you a commission every time they consume or use the service provided by the network company you are with. Diversifying your sources of income in this manner is a risk management strategy that is necessary to protect income generation potential.

• Flexibility

You are not limited by time and location. You have the flexibility to work with whomever you want and whenever you want. A network marketing business can be done part-time or full-time.

• Personal growth

Growing a team and your income in network marketing is all about personal growth. Jim Rohn once said your income will seldom exceed personal development. This means the more you grow as a person the bigger your income becomes. Network marketing companies are big on personal development and growth. As a leader in network marketing you must build your people and help them to become better people. So, coaching is a core competence for network marketing leaders.

• Residual or/and passive Income

Network marketing is the best business model to give you residual or even passive residual income. Network marketing can liberate you from the time-for-money trap i.e. the trading of hours for Rands (linear income). In this trap if you are not working you are not earning. This is not how you get wealthy and attain time freedom. Network marketing affords you the ability to do something well once and get paid over and over again for your efforts, proving an income stream that is residual and passive. Warren Buffett once said: "if you do not find a way to make money while you sleep, you will work until you die."

• Unlimited income potential

The income potential in network marketing is huge. Les Brown records that network marketing has produced more millionaires than any other industry in the history of the world.

• No employees: Low management control

This means network marketing has lower management control compared to other business models. This business model has no payroll matters to manage or industrial relations complications like you would have in a traditional business. In network marketing you will not deal with strikes or union demands. All this means the cost of running your network marketing business is much lower than the cost of operating a traditional or even a franchise business.

• No billing or accounts receivable

In a network marketing business you do not have to worry about billing any of your customers, or collecting any money. That is all handled by the company you have a contract with. In a traditional business sometimes you can wait for 60 to 90 days to collect your money. In network marketing you will not have working capital issues.

- ## Financial security

The South African labour market is very unstable. Almost all adverse economic events end up with retrenchments or a downward adjustment of salaries and wages. Having a conventional job offers extraordinarily little financial security. David Wood calls a job – "Just Over Broke". Even high-paying jobs are susceptible to retrenchments, with the shrinking job market and technological advancements leading to fewer and fewer people needed to do the same job as there once was. That is why it is important to have multiple streams of income and to dig your well before you are thirsty. A network marketing business is more secure and stable compared to a job.

- ## Getting poorer with rising prices – inflation

Salary and wage increase often lag real inflation. With such increases it means each year employees are getting poorer. In network marketing it is possible to double your income each year. It is impossible to double your income year-on-year with a job.

- ## Build your own fortune, not your boss's

In a network marketing business, you are building your own fortune. In a job situation you are only making a meagre living and your boss is making a fortune out of your blood, sweat and tears.

- ## True financial freedom

One of the main reasons people get into network marketing is the need to attain financial freedom. This means a state where you can earn lots of money without needing to be there. With a job you will be locked in contractually in a 40-40 time-for-money trap. A lot of people never get to enjoy financial and time freedom, because they must sell 40 hours of their time per week for 40 years to get money. These people never stop working because their income will also stop. With network marketing you will have a guaranteed stream of income whether you are there or not. As we all know the 9 – 5 is broken. So many people will be retrenched in their lifetime. This means there is no security in a job. Network marketing is the best business model or profession to create residual income and to attain true financial freedom.

Why Network Marketing is the Great Business of the Future

Network marketing gives people from all walks of life a chance to develop their own income-generating assets with low financial commitment and low risk. Jim Collins says

"Network marketing offers the most systematic way for the ordinary individual to achieve economic success". Network marketing companies provide network marketing entrepreneurs with all the support, tools, infrastructure, and training that is needed to run a successful business. In network marketing the break-even period is much shorter compared to a traditional business and you earn while you learn the ropes of the business. In network marketing you are in business for yourself but not by yourself. This industry is often described as the business model of the future. Network marketing allows entrepreneurs to create a substantial residual income stream in part-time or full-time hours with potential for exponential growth for generational wealth. Further, here are some of the features of network marketing that qualify it to fit the future-proof business model:

- In network marketing your will get a golden opportunity to build your own fortune, not someone else's.

- The potential to grow your income exponentially. Network marketing income can build itself.

- You can run your business in the comfort of your home and with the ease of your cell phone.

- With network marketing you can live a rich and rewarding life regardless of your background.

- Through passive residual income you will enjoy security of income.

- You can enjoy financial freedom and time freedom that will allow you to retire early.

Network marketing has imbedded in it the following future-fit characteristics:

- Learning ethos.
- Distributed decision-making.
- Self-organising and locally-attuning.
- Value-creation for all participants.
- Empowerment: Prosperous future for all.
- Inspirational.
- Interconnected.
- Regenerative.

Top Reasons Why Some Network Marketers Fail

- Failure to prospect correctly and to attract good-quality entrepreneurs. Lack of leads is a real challenge for some network marketers.

- Lack of ambition and commitment to the business. Most network marketers do not invest in personal development and they do not build sustainable teams. These network entrepreneurs run their businesses with an employee mindset. With any big venture, there will be an equal or greater amount of effort and work put in to reap the rewards. If you want to earn six-figures in your business, you will need to be willing to put in whatever it takes to reach that financial goal.

- Too income driven. Most people join the business and limit their focus to only making big money. These network marketers only set they eyes on monetary gains. They view prospects as walking ATM machines and not potential entrepreneurs and team leaders. The fundamental mantra of network marketing is that: **One cannot succeed without helping others to succeed first**. If you are not a natural nurturer of potential, you will never see sustained growth and success in network marketing.

- Lack of excitement. In network marketing it is critical to have a strong sense of desire and to be excited about what the future holds. Remembering your WHY will keep you going even in the face of challenges.

- Easily discouraged. People who are quitters do not make it in network marketing.

- The Salesman Mentality: Network marketers are not salespeople. A salesperson's job is to close the sale, get commission, move on the next sale, and let the company's customer service agents worry about the rest. Their key focus is on signing up people. This is a hunter modus operandi. On the other hand, successful network marketers focus on duplicating themselves. Like farmers, successful network marketers nurture the talents of distributors they recruit into the business. Network marketing is about leveraging your time and efforts instead of doing everything yourself.

- Lack of proper marketing training. Some network marketing companies do not equip their marketers. Network marketers must invest in their development. Even if you are a seasoned business owner, you will probably learn that network marketing is different from traditional businesses. Jim Rohn once said, "Income will seldom exceed self-development." Self-development is critical if you are to have a successful and sustainable business.

- Lack of duplication. This challenge manifests where 90% of a network marketer's earnings come from his or her own effort and not from the efforts of their downline. Here are a few tips for establishing duplication in network marketing:

    ◆ Set a good example for your downline.

    ◆ Get your team started correctly.

    ◆ Help your team members to set up a Daily Method of Operation.

Network Marketing is Big Business

Network marketing is a big industry and its performance speaks for itself. This industry has grown at an exponential rate. More and more families are creating extra income through network marketing. Network marketing is a perfect vehicle for today's entrepreneur. This industry provides a perfect opportunity for millions of people take full responsibility for their financial success and to create wealth. There are more than 66 million network marketing entrepreneurs globally. David Wood on the Network Marketing Documentary 2020 says, 82 out of 100 women in North America who earn over $100,000 a year, are professional network marketers. According to Direct Selling Mastermind Event.com here is how the network marketing industry grew between 2012 and 2013 compared to major industries in the US:

2013	2012
Professional Football League: $9.58 Billion	Professional Football League: $9.5 Billion
Music Industry: $15 Billion	Music Industry: $16.5 Billion
Movie Industry: $88 Billion	Movie Industry: $80 Billion
Video Gaming Industry: $76 Billion	Video Gaming Industry: $67 Billion
Natural Food Industry: $90 Billion	Organic Products: $91 Billion
Network Marketing: $178 Billion	Network Marketing: $167 Billion

The above table clearly shows that network marketing is big business. It has created more millionaires that any other industry in the history of this world. Eric Worre says, "network marketing isn't perfect, it is just better".

According to Art Jonak, 2017 was a breakout year. The number of network marketing distributors grew to 116 million and sales grew to $189 billion – both record highs. The network marketing industry grew by 27% between 2012 to 2017. Most distributors start off as part-time hustlers and soon realise that there is a proper chance of building a viable business in network marketing.

Chapter 6

My Network Marketing Journey

"If you don't have any residual or passive income,
or at least a plan for residual income, you are living
a very risky life."

—Ray Hidgon

In 2001 I was a Deputy CEO of a small medical aid company in Durban. Even though I was a high net earner it was clear to me that my active income was not enough to finance my dreams and purpose in life. Consequently, I started looking for business opportunities to help me diversify my income sources. T.D. Jakes, bishop, author and filmmaker, once said, "Stop expecting your job to fund your vision. Your vision is bigger than your pay cheque."

It became clear to me early in my executive career that my pay cheque will never make me wealthy. As a single parent I wanted to give my daughter the absolute best life has to offer. I wanted to send her to best schools and I wanted to be able to expose her to international travel at an early age. My quest for a better life forced me to look for business opportunities that would help me to create multiple streams of income so that I could finance my dreams and aspirations. It was important to me that one of those streams should give me residual income. Residual income is income that continues to be generated after the initial effort has been expanded.

In July 2001, a friend of mine invited me to a Clientele Life business opportunity meeting. Clientele Life was looking for network marketers that would sign up as Independent Field Advertisers. Unlike insurance brokers, IFAs advertise Clientele Life products through network marketing. When the IFA business opportunity was unpacked, I saw it as a business opportunity where my business could improve on a daily basis, where my income would increase monthly and where I could earn monthly bonuses. A big advantage of this business model is that I didn't need a lot of capital upfront. I saw this opportunity as a no-risk venture. This opportunity presented me with many incredible benefits such as flexibility of running my business part-time or full-time, unlimited income potential, free training, and a whole lot more.

What Attracted Me to Network Marketing

- The IFA business model is based on a referral system. In the IFA business we get paid for marketing business opportunity meetings. If prospects attend these meetings and join the business by taking up a financial product with the company, you make money that way.

- There are no joining fees, or upfront fees.

- The right to receive rewards is not linked to the level of stock you need to buy and sell.

- There are no samples that distributors must buy and no cash flow that is tied up in company products.

- The capacity of the business model to create residual income is unlimited.

I worked and built a strong team for a year between June and July 2001. My first earnings were a meagre R141.00. I attained Club 27 within 4 months and within 10 months of working the business part-time I achieved Club 250. In August of 2002, I moved to Cape Town to join Old Mutual. It became difficult for me to build my network marketing business from Cape Town. For that reason I became dormant in my IFA business for 17 years while I was building my corporate career. A career that has afforded me the privilege of serving at board level and in many JSE listed companies such as Massmart, South32 (former BHP Billiton), Pick n Pay, Tongaat Hulett and Aspen Pharmacare. During the same period, I had the privilege of serving as the Chairperson of the Wholesale and Retail SETA Board. I also had the privilege of serving on the Council of the University of Zululand where I chaired the HR and Remuneration sub-committee of Council and have also had the privilege of serving on the Advisory Boards of GIBS and UJ as well as guest-lecturing at UKZN Graduate School of Business on the MBA programme where I was an external examiner for several years. During the 17 years, I built a strong corporate career while I continued to enjoy a passive residual income of over R4 million from my IFA business. Others call residual income "walk-away money". The quality of the team that you build in network marketing will determine how sustainable your business will be over time.

As a strong believer in multiple streams of income, I used my IFA earnings to set up my property investment portfolio. I would not have been able to do this without the passive residual income I was enjoying from my network marketing business. Passive income is income that requires little or no effort to earn and maintain. Residual income is important and if some of your residual income could be passive income, you have struck gold. Residual income in network marketing is income you continue to earn based on efforts you put forth initially. I now enjoy passive residual income from my property portfolio and my network marketing business.

I am now a full-time coach in network marketing. My key focus is on coaching up and coming network marketing entrepreneurs and high-performing teams. I strongly believe network marketing is the gateway to entrepreneurship.

Chapter 7

Misconceptions About Network Marketing

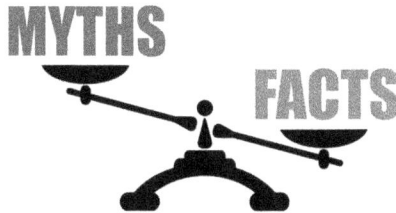

MYTHS

FACTS

"You will meet people who believe network marketing opportunities are pyramid schemes. Why spend all your time trying to convince them otherwise when there are legions of people who are open to what you have?"

—Randy Gage

The benefits of network marketing over a job or start-up or franchise businesses are there for all to see. There is ample empirical evidence that network marketing has created more millionaires than any other industry in the world. So, why are people not flocking to this industry? It is a proven fact that network marketing has produced many South Africans who earn five-figure monthly earnings. This status can be achieved by anyone who is prepared to work hard. To be a high earner it is important for you to understand this highly lucrative industry and to run your business as a professional.

The first misconception is that network marketing is just like a pyramid scheme. In my view this is because people do not understand the difference between a network marketing business model and the illegal pyramid schemes that continue to scam a lot of desperate people. Let us examine the nature of pyramid schemes:

What is a Pyramid Scheme?

A pyramid is a business model that recruits members via a promise of payment for enrolling others into the scheme, rather than the sale of goods or services. In such fraudulent schemes, profits are based on recruiting an ever-increasing number of investors. The initial promoters recruit investors who, in turn, recruit more investors. Notably, there is no product or service that exchanges hands.

Pyramid schemes are scams. They can look remarkably like legitimate network marketing business opportunities, but if you become a distributor for a pyramid scheme, it can cost you and your recruits a substantial amount of money.

Multi-Level Marketing vs Pyramid Schemes

The difference between a **pyramid scheme** and a lawful **MLM** program is that there is no real product that is sold in a **pyramid scheme**. Participants attempt to make money solely by recruiting new participants into the programme.

The promoters of a pyramid scheme may try to recruit you with promises of what you will earn. These schemes sell a promise of a better life. They promise that you can change your life by recruiting people who will make financial contributions to the company. Your income would be based on how many people you recruit, not how much product or services you sell. Pyramid schemes are set up to encourage recruitment to keep a constant stream of new recruits – and their money – flowing into the business. South Africa has seen a fair share of such schemes. They generally leave a trail of destruction behind. People normally lose everything.

Other pyramid schemes imitate network marketing companies very closely. Here are some signs that often distinguish pyramids from normal network marketing companies:

- In a pyramid scheme, you will be encouraged or even required to buy a certain amount of product at regular intervals, even if you already have more inventory than you can use or sell.

- You may even have to buy products before you are eligible to be paid or get certain bonuses. You may also have to pay high fees for other items, like training sessions or expensive marketing materials.

- In addition, the company may say you can earn lavish rewards, like prizes, bonuses, exotic vacations, and luxury cars. However, it often turns out that you must meet certain product purchase, recruitment, training, or other goals to qualify for the rewards, and only a handful of distributors ever qualify.

- Eventually, most distributors find that no matter how hard they work, they cannot sell enough inventory or recruit enough people to make money. They also cannot keep up with required fees or the inventory purchases they need to make to qualify for rewards, and they cannot earn enough money to cover their expenses. In the end, most people run out of money, they quit, and lose everything they invested.

Here are some warning signs of a pyramid scheme:

- Promoters make over-the-top promises about your earning potential. Such promises are false. If it sounds too good to be true it probably is.

- Your earnings are based mainly on the number of people you recruit, and the money those new recruits pay to join the scheme – not the sales of a product or service.

- Promoters play on your emotions or use high-pressure sales tactics, maybe saying you will lose the opportunity if you do not act now and discouraging you from taking time to study the company. Be warned, do not join under pressure.

- Distributors are forced to buy lots more inventory than they want to use or can resell, just to stay active in the company or to qualify for bonuses or other rewards. If you see this happening, do not get involved.

In such schemes, recruiting becomes quickly impossible and most members are unable to profit as such pyramid schemes are unsustainable and often illegal. Such schemes are not registered with industry bodies that regulate network marketing companies such as the Direct Selling Association of South Africa.

The second misconception is that network marketing is a get-rich-quick scheme. Like any business, network marketing takes time to grow. It takes dedication and hard work to build a sustainable business in network marketing.

The third misconception is that network marketing is so simple that anyone can do it. Nothing could be further from the truth. Network marketing has a low barrier to entry and this is attractive to many people. The fact is that even though network marketing is accessible to everyone, it is not everyone who makes it in this business. To enjoy success in network marketing, you must be prepared to put in time and hard work. Even those network marketers who are doing the business part-time must put in 100% effort. In network marketing you get exactly what you put in. Network marketing favours hard work.

The fourth misconception is that the only way to make it in network marketing is to sign up your family, friends, and neighbours. In network marketing this is your warm marketing. If you only rely on your warm market you will not grow a sustainable business. The list of people you know will soon run out. Successful network marketers have strategies of attracting people outside their circle of friends and family. There are proven ways of generating leads that will ensure profitability of your business.

Chapter 8

Corporate Governance and Ethics in Network Marketing

"Within the realm of network marketing there is no room for any interaction that ends in someone losing."

—Stephen Covey

How to Choose the Right Network Marketing Company

Governance and ethics are important in the successful running of a successful network marketing business. There are many network marketing companies that are legit and that have helped thousands of people to get ahead in life. Here is a simple checklist that you can use to determine the legitimacy of a network marketing company:

- Look at how long the company has been in business.

- Examine the management team.

- Search the internet to see if the company has any lawsuits or outstanding complaints against it.

- Analyse the product or services you will be marketing. Here you will be looking to see if there is no potential values clash between what you stand for and what the company does. Further, check if there is a demand for products and services that are rendered by the company.

- Examine the compensation plan. Check whether you will be compensated for just bringing in investors or whether there is a product or service that will exchange hands.

- Determine the amount of help you will get with marketing.

- Consider the training and support you will be receiving.

- Search for testimonies from high earners in the company. Check to see if the company delivers on its brand promise.

- Check to see if the company is a member of the Direct Selling Association (DSA). If the company is in the financial services space, check whether the company is registered with the Financial Services Conduct Authority.

Why Is the Direct Selling Association Important?

Belonging to an association with an established reputation of vetting its member companies' compensations plans, compliance to its Code of Ethics and compliance to the laws of South Africa, lends legitimacy and credibility to the operations of the network marketing company and the distributors that are affiliated with it. The Direct Selling Association of South Africa (DSA) is a national business association founded in 1972. This association represents member direct selling/network marketing companies that distribute goods and services through independent contractors or distributors directly to consumers, away from a fixed retail location.

DSA is a self-regulating association of direct selling/network marketing companies that promotes and protects the interest of member companies who passionately create an enabling environment in which lives are positively changed in our country. Every DSA member company pledges to abide by the terms as set out in the industry Code of Ethics as a condition of admission and continuing membership of the Direct Selling Association of South Africa. All direct sellers or network marketing entrepreneurs are also bound by the DSA's Code of Ethics when representing a DSA member company.

The Code of Conduct of the DSA has been developed within the framework and requirements of the World Federation of Direct Selling Associations (WFDSA) Code of Ethics.

Current members of the DSA are listed alphabetically as follows:

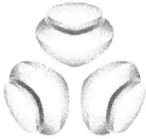

AFFINITY BUSINESS NETWORK

Contact Person: Monique Delport
Telephone: 0861 111 755
Fax: 086 6000 536
Email: monique@affinitybn.co.za
Website: https://www.affinitybn.co.za/

Affinity Business Network offers a business opportunity to all South Africans who want to create financial freedom by earning an extra income through marketing, advertising & promoting the Affinity Suite of products.

AIM AFRICA INC. (Health Supplements)
Contact Person: Leanda Mostert
Telephone: 011 675 0477
Fax: 011 675 0427
Email: lmostert@aimintl.com
Website: http://www.theaimcompanies.com/

AMC COOKWARE (Cookware, Cutlery)
Contact Person: Clare Hendry
Telephone: 086 111 1262
Fax: 021 797 5092
Email: info@amcsa.co.za
Website: https://www.amcsa.co.za/en/home/

AMWAY SOUTH AFRICA (Beauty, Health and Wellness, Home,
Personal, Durables)
Contact Person: Rajesh Parshotam
Telephone: 011 201 4400
Fax: 011 201 4401
Email: raj_parshotam@amway.co.za
Website: https://www.amway.co.za/en/a2kWeb/

ANNIQUE HEALTH AND BEAUTY (Health and Beauty Products)
Contact Person: Annalie Grobbelaar
Telephone: 012 345 9800
Fax: 012 345 9854
Email: annalie.grobbelaar@annique.com
Website: http://www.annique.com/

ASCENDIS HEALTH DIRECT (Nutritional/Health Products,
Household Products and Personal Care)
Contact Person: Theo Meyer
Telephone: 011 317 8300
Fax: 011 317 8400
Email: danadee@sportron.co.za
Website: http://www.ascendisdirect.com/

AVON JUSTINE (Cosmetics, Personal Care, Fashion & Home)
Contact Person: Mafahle Mareletse
Telephone: 010 205 5000
Email: queries@avon.com
Website: https://my.avon.co.za/
https://my.justine.co.za/About-Justine/

BOTLE BUHLE
BRANDS

BOTLE BUHLE BRANDS
Contact Person: Dave Perlstein
Telephone: 010 442 0222
Fax: 086 552 8508
Email: dave@bbb.co.za
Website: https://bbb.co.za

Home, Beauty, Health and Wellness, Fashion

CANYON ORGANICS

CANYON ORGANICS (Health Food Supplements, Personal Care, Cleaning Products)
Contact Person: Norman Fels
Telephone: 011 886 2932
Fax: 011 886 3047
Email: nfels@happi.co.za
Website: http://www.canyon.co.za/

DUEPOINT

DUEPOINT (Insurance & Lifestyle Products)
Contact Person: Brendan Benfield
Telephone: 010 020 4500
Email: info@duepoint.net
Website: https://www.duepoint.net/

E**D**MARK®

EDMARK DIRECT MARKETING RSA (Multi-level Marketing)
Contact Person: Maricar L Granada
Telephone: 071 109 0350
Email: maricargranada@edmarker.com
Website: https://edmarker.com/v2/

FOREVER
LIVING PRODUCTS

FOREVER LIVING PRODUCTS (Homecare, Healthcare, Weight Loss, Skin Care)
Contact Person: Richard Beeton
Telephone: 021 761 6001
Fax: 021 761 4271
Email: rick@forever.co.za
Website: http://www.foreverliving.com

HERBALIFE NUTRITION

HERBALIFE NUTRITION (Weight Management, Wellness, Fit & Active and Personal Care)
Contact Person: Tanya Clague
Telephone: 011 554 1000
Fax: 086 480 7059
Email: tanyacl@herbalife.com
Website: https://www.herbalife.co.za/

for the home you love

HOMECHOICE (Bedding, Blankets, Appliances, Kitchen & Dining,
Furniture, Fashion)
Contact Person: Rose Gxowa
Telephone: 086 199 9635
Email: rgxowa@homechoice.co.za
Website: https://www.homechoice.co.za/direct-sales-agent

IFA/CLIENTELE LIFE (Insurance)
Contact Person: Yurika Pistorius
Telephone: 011 320 3471
Email: ypistorius@clientele.co.za
Website: http://www.ifa.co.za/

JEUNESSE (Spray Vitamins)
Contact Person: Jared Thwaits
Telephone: 010 500 6961
Email: jared.thwaits@jeunessehq.com
Website: https://www.jeunesseglobal.com/

MANNATECH (Nutritional Supplements, Skin Care, Fat Loss & Fitness, Home Living)
Contact Person: Elizabeth Strydom
Telephone: 011 615 0188
Fax: 011 615 8750
Email: info@mannatechsa.com
Website: https://www.mannatech.com/

NEOLIFE INTERNATIONAL (Whole Food Nutritional Supplements, Weight Management, Golden Home Care, Organic Skin Care)
Contact Person: Pieter de Bruin
Telephone: 011 409 3000
Email: Info.Johannesburg@za.neolife.com
Website: https://www.neolife.com

NU SKIN ENTERPRISE SA (Anti-Aging, Cosmetics & Dietary Supplements)
Contact Person: Nicola Coleman
Telephone: 087 550 3103
Email: ncoleman@nuskin.com
Website: https://www.nuskin.com/nuskin.html

PRES LES (Quality Home Products)
Contact Person: Lise De Kock
Telephone: 021 672 3100
Email: info@presles.co.za
Website: http://www.presles.co.za/

SH'ZEN

SH'ZEN (Skin Care, Cosmetics, Make-up, Personal Care Goods)
Contact Person: Ingrid
Telephone: 021 704 2940
Fax: 021 704 2941
Email: Ingrid@shzen.co.za
Website: http://shzen.co.za/shzen/index.php

Stemtech

STEMTECH AFRICA (Natural Adult Stem Cell Enhancers)
Contact Person: Faizal Razack
Telephone: 011 803 3633
Fax: 086 616 5144
Email: frazack@stemtech.com
Website: http://www.stemtech.com

TABLE CHARM (Tableware, Fine Fragrances, Personal Care, Jewellery & Handbags)
Contact Person: Angelique van Wyk
Telephone: 011 226 1600
Fax: 086 614 9890
Email: siza@tablecharm.co.za
Website: https://www.tablecharm.co.za/

THE ART OF SKIN CARE (Cosmeceutical Products)
Contact Person: Desmond Ngobeni
Telephone: 011 804 7550
Fax: 011 804 3666
Email: hdngobeni@artofskincare.co.za
Website: http://artofskincare.co.za/shop/

TIANSHI SA (TIENS) (Traditional Chinese Health Care)
Contact Person: Yusuf Bhyat
Telephone: 011 787 5452
Fax: 011 787 8310
Email: yusuf@tiens.co.za
Website: www.tiens.com

Network marketers and members of the public at large are warned not to deal with companies that do not appear on this list. As stated, the Direct Selling Association is committed to the highest ethical business standards for the direct selling companies and for customers that they serve daily. The Code of Ethics protects consumers and independent distributors with standards that ensure members companies are held accountable when it comes to claims about earnings, products, and other important areas.

Chapter 9

Winning with Network Marketing

"An entrepreneur with strong networks makes money even when he is asleep".
—Amit Kalantri

Network marketing is not a get-rich-quick scheme. This business model will only produce results when consistent work is put in. In network we say there is no secret to success, but there is a system to success. There are a few key principles that must be observed by network marketing entrepreneurs to achieve sustainable success and to enjoy all the rewards that are inherent in this highly profitable business model. These key principles are listed below:

Seven Rs That Determine Success in Network Marketing

1. You must choose the **right company**. The first step is to make sure you get in with the right company.

2. You must have the **right spirit** – entrepreneurial spirit. You cannot win in network marketing if you run your business with an employee mindset.

3. You must choose the **right business coach**.

4. You must have the **right expectations**. You must be prepared to work your business. You must give your business 100% effort even if you are running your business part-time. You must be all in. You do not flirt with entrepreneurship. Commitment is important in this business model.

5. You must have the **right attitude**. This means to succeed in network marketing you must be coachable and teachable. If you do not stop learning you will never stop earning.

6. You must choose the **right people**. As you build your team you must recruit people who are entrepreneurs who have the mentality of entrepreneurs and not the employee mindset. Remember, iron sharpens iron. You cannot grow a team of ducks and eagles in one stable. If you want to build a sustainable team, recruit and coach eagles. Spend 80% of your time nurturing eagles. The heights you will reach, and the long-term sustainability of your network marketing business depend largely on the strength and quality of your team. So, if you are going to excel in this business you must perfect the art of recruiting eagles. Remember, ducks only make noise. They have no vision for the future, and they cannot fly.

7. It is critical to have the **right system** in network marketing. As a leader it is important for you to create simple duplicatable practices that your team can follow to build their teams. A simple daily method of operation will facilitate duplication in your business.

Following the above principles will create massive momentum for your business. These principles will ensure that new recruits get started correctly in the business. The above truths will also help you to grow leaders in your business. Further, this process will be a blueprint to multiplication and duplication in your business.

Income Producing Activities (IPA) That Drive Success in Network Marketers

All successful network marketers have mastered the following critical skills and competencies. Further, they build these income-producing activities into a daily method of operation. Consistency in executing these activities is critical for massive and sustainable results:

- **Prospecting and developing a list of leads.** Successful network marketers use the internet to run massive prospecting campaigns. Prospecting online helps to ensure that you attract people that are already looking for what you have to offer instead of you chasing down your family, friends, and colleagues.

- **Inviting leads to view your business opportunity.** This could either be an invite to your business opportunity meeting or you could invite your prospect to watch third-party tools such as a video.

- **Presenting your opportunity.** It is important for you to be able to give an effective presentation of your business opportunity. This means you must understand the product and the business opportunity that you are offering your prospect. Generally, network marketing presentations will include a brief overview of the company, products/services, compensation plan and the testimonials of successful people in the business. It is important for network marketers to master the skill of presenting.

- **Follow-up.** After inviting people to look at your network marketing opportunity, follow-up is especially important. In network marketing we say money is in the follow-up. Most people do not follow up because they do not want to get negative feedback. Follow-up is a skill that successful network marketers must master.

- **Closing the deal.** The definition of closing in network marketing is simply to help prospects to sign on the dotted line. Your network marketing business will grow exponentially if you are skilled and competent at closing prospects. This activity seals the deal. Closing properly can mean the difference between winning the business and not.

- **Coaching new recruits.** Effective coaching leads to duplication in network marketing. All top network marketers are good at training people to become successful in network marketing.

All the above income-producing activities will force successful network marketers to be serious about their own personal development. Perfecting the income-producing activities can make you a substantial amount of money.

Automation in Network Marketing

"If your business is not on the internet, then your business will be out of business."
—Bill Gates

Most of the above income-producing activities can now be fully automated. Historically, most high earners in network marketing had to work extremely hard to establish and grow their income levels. In the days of e-commerce and internet, growing and maintaining your network marketing income does not have to be equivalent to modern-day slavery with zero time-freedom and autonomy. It is possible to scale your network marketing income through technology. The days of person-to-person prospecting and inviting, person-to-person presentation, person-to-person training and person-to-person enrolment or signing up are slowly becoming a thing of the past.

Automation is taking network marketing by storm. The days of traditional network marketing manual work are soon going to be history. The entire network marketing from lead generation to closing and signing up can be fully automated. Even person-to-person training and coaching is being replaced by online training and development. Exciting days are here for the network marketing industry. A lot of network marketers are already using platforms such as Facebook and LinkedIn for prospecting and inviting people to view their business opportunities. You can now automate the qualification process for high-quality prospects. This process will allow you to sort through and get to the serious prospects that are worth your time and only follow up with those prospects.

Most network marketing companies already have third-party tools that are fully automated. This will assist network marketers to automate their businesses easily.

Types of Network Marketing Entrepreneurs

People who are willing to work hard and put in constant effort are considered h**ustler entrepreneurs**. They often start small and work toward growing a bigger business with hard work rather than capital. Their aspirations are what motivates them, and they are willing to do what it takes to achieve their goals. They do not give up easily and are willing to experience challenges to get what they want. Network marketing falls into this category of entrepreneurship. In my view there are three types of network marketing entrepreneurs:

- Builders
- Ducks and
- Consumers

What differentiates the three types of network marketing entrepreneurs is their focus and approach (mindset); and their skills and competencies.

- **Builders:** These are **eagles**. Like eagles, builders in network marketing have powerful vision and they are fearless. Eagles are tenacious. Network marketing has ups and downs like all businesses. Eagles in network marketing use the storms of life to rise to greater height. High achievers thrive on challenges and use them profitably. Most importantly, eagles are highflyers and they nurture their young. Builders or eagles focus on the long-term. They focus on recruiting and nurturing hustler entrepreneurs. Builders spend a considerable amount of time learning about the network marketing industry in general and the specific company they have partnered with. They understand that their income is dependent on their level of self-development. Hence builders will invest in themselves and ensure that they improve their skills and competencies. They also instil the same way of working in their teams. Builders are great coaches to their teams. They produce and lead other leaders. This approach of builders creates duplication within their organisation. This leads to the development of multiple levels of generations. Hence the term "multi-level marketing". Builders approach their network marketing businesses as a profession. They behave like farmers. They nurture sound business relationships with their prospects first and with the teams they lead. Builders understand that in network marketing leaders build teams and teams in turn will build sustainable businesses.

- **Ducks:** These network marketers have all the features of an eagle, but they never fly. Peter Drucker once said, "If you want to fly with the eagles, you have to stop swimming with the ducks." He went on to say, "Ducks quack and complain while eagles soar above clouds and the crowd." This is also true in network marketing. Ducks in network marketing are weak and they fall behind in ability and achievement. These ducks behave like hunters inside a network marketing business. They want to shoot to kill and enjoy the spoils for that moment. These are people who are normally looking for extra cash for their immediate needs. I would call these lame ducks "Chancers". Dr Denis Waitley once said: "The secret is to take control of your future by choice instead of chance." They have no long-term vision for their businesses. They do not invest in self-development and they also do not develop their teams. Lame ducks do not build sustainable businesses. They are forever focused on bringing in new people. Unlike eagles, ducks do not nurture their recruits. Their focus is on bringing in new consumers who may not convert to distributors. So, their focus is not on building teams. Lame ducks lead followers. They typically do not produce leaders of leaders. They do not nurture teams and duplication is exceedingly difficult under the leadership of lame ducks.

- **Consumers** in a network marketing business. They are end users of company products and services. They got into the business with no intention to work the business. They do not have entrepreneurial aspirations. They joined because they like the products or services and they trust the company. These people typically do not even attend business opportunity meetings and other company events. They are just loyal consumers of the products or services. Some consumers do not actually believe in the business opportunity that the network marketing company is offering. Other consumers may not believe in the potential of network marketing to generate revenue or even to create wealth. Others are just too lazy to work.

As an entrepreneur if you want to run a profitable and sustainable network marketing business, target builders in your prospecting and recruitment campaigns.

The System of Success in Network Marketing

Success favours **Builders** in network marketing. Very few **Lame Ducks** or **Consumers** make it as entrepreneurs in network marketing. People often ask me to share my secret of success in network marketing. From the very get go I would like to submit that there is no secret of success, there is only a system of success.

There are numerous reasons why some network marketing entrepreneurs fail. The failure to build width and depth in their business structures ranks number one among those reasons. Building width in your key appointments or your level one will give you profitability and depth which refers to the levels that are brought in by your key appointments and the generations below them will ensure sustainability of your business. Both width and depth are largely driven by the quality of network marketing entrepreneurs in your business. The results you get in your network marketing business will depend on the quality of your recruits and the quality of coaching you provide for your teams. Therefore, to enjoy sustainable profitability you need to master the skill of identifying network marketing entrepreneurs and the skill of coaching your teams for superior performance.

The tried and tested system of success for network marketing entrepreneurs is the following:

- Choose to be an entrepreneur. You will not succeed in network marketing if you approach your business with an employee mindset. Put in 100% effort even if you are still doing it part-time.

- Believe in the products or services you will be marketing.

- Invest in personal development – leadership development and related technical skills such as prospecting, inviting, follow-up, closing and coaching for performance.

- Recruit other entrepreneurs. Remember, you will never get gold from coal. So, if you recruit consumers, do not expect them to build teams. Entrepreneurship is not about owning a business, but rather, entrepreneurship is a mindset.

- Invest in your team. Coaching and training are critical.

In conclusion, there are five network marketing tips for **explosive and sustained growth:**

- Choose the right network marketing company.

- Dedicate your time wisely.

- Spend time doing only revenue-generating activities.

- Leverage the internet/online to build your business.

- Coach and train as many people as possible.

Chapter 10

The Role of Coaching in Network Marketing

"Your level of success will seldom exceed your
level of personal development."
—Jim Rohn

The life blood of network marketing is duplication. Going alone is not an option in the network marketing business. The behaviour that facilitates duplication in network marketing is coaching. Coaching is a performance-enhancement initiative. Every leader in network marketing must have a coach and every leader must be a coach to the people they lead. Like with any business, coaching is critical for network marketing business success. Coaching is a space where you can explore, develop, and nurture your options and opportunities. It focuses on meeting specific objectives within a set period and is meant to enhance performance and develop certain skills and behaviours.

Who is Coaching For?

- Coaching is right for everyone who wants to improve his or her performance.

- Coaching is for people who want to supercharge and take their business to the next level.

- It creates a safe space to express, plan and reimagine.

- It is important for leaders as they navigate personal uncertainties and ambiguous situations.

- It is important for new network entrepreneurs who are unfamiliar with the network marketing business model.

What is Business Coaching?

A business coach will assist and guide the network marketing business owner in running a business by helping them clarify the vision of their business and how it fits in with their personal goals and values. Coaching in network marketing supports new recruits and fast tracks high-potential networkers to the top. Business coaching is a process used to take a business from where it is now to where the business owner wants it to be. Advantages of this process include:

- Crystal-clear goal setting. Business coaches help protégés to build actionable plans. A coach will help you see the bigger picture.

- Creation of owner accountability: Monthly business coaching sessions help protégés maintain accountability and focus on setting goals and meeting them. You will learn how to make your ideas a reality.

- Better focus through fruitful brainstorming. A coach will be your sounding board.

- Personal development. You will gain self-confidence.

- Improved profitability. Business coaching creates business growth. Network marketers will climb the ladder faster.

- Objective performance feedback. A coach will tell it like it is – even if you do not like it. You will get unbiased opinions.

- As a protégé you will get personal attention from someone who knows your business inside out.

Coaching and Network Marketing Sponsor

In network marketing the role of a coach is often played by the sponsor or upline. A sponsor or an upline is someone who introduced you the network marketing business. The basic role of a sponsor or your upline is to help you get started with your business. A good network marketing sponsor will coach you on the ways to follow if you want your business to grow and succeed.

Network marketing sponsors are there to coach you and not to do the work for you. Your sponsor will guide you on how to manage the following income-generating activities of your business:

- Inviting prospects: cold and warm markets.
- Training.
- Scheduling appointments.
- Obtaining business tools.

A coach or a sponsor in network marketing would hold your hand through the above activities to get you started in the business until you are able to run on your own. It is not the responsibility of your coach/sponsor to run your business for you. Your sponsor will always be available for you should you need guidance even in the advanced stages of your business. You may hold joint events with your sponsor/ coach, for instance. In the network marketing industry people say: 'You are in business for yourself but not by yourself.' You are always surrounded by coaches from your upline and from the company.

In summary, coaches render the following functions:

- Give advice.

- Provide guidance.

- Provide support.

- Give confidence.

- Promote greater competence and skills.

Coaching will also help you to:

- Bolster your individual resilience and wellbeing.

- Adapt to your fast-changing environment.

- Explore new ideas.

- Reprioritise your business agenda.

- Maintain team cohesion in tough times.

- Coaching will also help to increase a networker's motivation and productivity.

Network marketers who receive effective coaching from their leaders (upline), increase their own ability to coach and develop their teams. Good coaching also increases the retention rate of network marketers. Coaching will help all network marketers or team members to improve the way they run their current businesses and increase their potential to do more in the future. Coaching is concerned about long-term sustainable performance of team members.

To build teams that are built-to-last in network marketing you need to:

Become a professional business coach. You need to know how to grow human potential through:

- Helping people become their best selves and great leaders.

- Coaching people to achieve personal, business and team goals.

- Engineering goal-focused performance conversations to help your protégés deliver breakthrough results.

How Does Coaching Work in Network Marketing?

There are five stages of coaching that network marketing leaders must follow:

- Help their downlines/teams identify specific goals and objectives: What they want to get out of their network marketing business.

- Assist protégés to objectively assess their current performance: How are they performing right now?

- Develop a performance improvement plan: Identify areas where performance improvement is needed.

- Assist downlines to develop a Daily Method of Operation: These are daily action steps that will lead to the achievement of the main goals.

- Ongoing feedback: As the protégé executes the plan, your role as the coach is to give objective and constructive feedback through evaluation and re-setting of goals.

Chapter 11

Gender Diversity in Network Marketing

$$♀♂$$

*"Network marketing is one of the few
places where women earn dollar for dollar
what men earn".*

—Art Jonak

Why is Network Marketing a Popular Business Model for Women?

Women in the South African labour market are caught in a cycle of vulnerability which is characterised by their retrenchment from full-time employment. More women are faced with economic hardships and challenges in corporates compared to their male counterparts. This gender inequality is costly for economies. In South Africa laws such as Broad-Based Black Economic Empowerment, the Gender Equality Act, the Employment Equity Act and the Skills Development Act all try to close the economic gender gap between men and women in the country. In spite of all these noble efforts, diversity and inclusion in the labour market landscape of South Africa is still a challenge. In the main women are still paid less than their male counterparts and more men than women lead in the C-Suite of most Johannesburg Stock Exchange Listed companies. There is still a need to create more gender equality in business to ensure access to top lucrative corporate positions for women.

Women are systematically discriminated against in corporates, especially after they take a break to build families. The inflexible work schedules are very limiting for most women who are raising families. Women are forced to make a choice between climbing the corporate ladder and spending quality time with their families. Network marketing offers women a solution to this challenge.

Five Reasons Women are Choosing Network Marketing

Having more control over their time, and more time for themselves and their families is one of the strongest motivators for women to start a network marketing business. Network marketing is one of the business models where women are not discriminated against in terms of access and income. Network marketing gives women a fair chance to embark on entrepreneurship and to become financially free. Here are some reasons why women are leaving the corporate world for network marketing:

- **Tired of the corporate grind and the corresponding risks.** The 40-40 time for cash trade is broken. Working 40 hours for 40 years is very limiting for women. This 40-40 trap comes with limited time and financial freedom. The traditional corporate jobs also entail the risk of producing inadequate pension funds at the end of the 40-year grind. The risk of retrenchments is another negative that is encouraging women to go into network marketing. Network marketing offers women a chance to own businesses and to enjoy unlimited income potential. This opportunity also comes with the ability to create residual income and to enjoy time freedom.

- **Opportunity to build and coach teams.** Network marketing allows women the opportunity to practise their natural abilities of building teams and nurturing talent. Success in network marketing comes from leveraged income. Hence the ability of the leader to recruit, develop and coach high performers is key. These are competencies that come naturally to most women. Women also enjoy the opportunity to collaborate and receive ongoing support from others in the team. Network marketing is a business for you, but not by yourself. It takes a team to succeed in network marketing. The isolation that most women suffer in the corporate world is not there in network marketing.

- **Opportunity to choose who you work with.** In network marketing women do not have to deal with ruthless bosses and cut-throat colleagues who are in it for themselves only. This can be a very liberating factor. In this business model, women will never suffer the discrimination that still prevails in many big corporates. As a network marketer you choose who you recruit to your team. This is truly liberating.

- **Necessity and financial security.** The economic meltdown and high retrenchment rate have forced more women to venture into entrepreneurship and to get into network marketing. The labour market is shrinking at a rapid rate, leaving people with no choice but to explore business opportunities. Due to low barriers to entry, low start-up costs and low monthly overheads, more and more women venture into network marketing. They enjoy the marketing and training support offered for free by most network marketing companies as well as the unlimited income potential that comes with this business model. They enjoy financial and time freedom that their corporate jobs were never going to offer them.

- **Recognition and rewards.** Unlike many corporates, network marketing companies make a huge effort to recognise and reward their distributors. Women enjoy greater rewards and incentives than they would enjoy in corporates. In network marketing women are paid according to their performance and not their gender. In network marketing there is a level playing field, where gender bias does not play a part in income or promotions. Network marketing is a merit-based income system. This levels the playing field and closes the pay gap that is still common in many corporate companies. More and more women are climbing the ladder in network marketing and they are making six- or seven-figure annual incomes. This is a great way for women to create wealth and time freedom. Art Jonak says network marketing is one of the few places where women earn dollar for dollar what men earn.

- **Low management control and flexibility.** High levels of support, free training and marketing support offered by network marketing companies, makes this model extremely attractive to women. Network marketing comes with low management control requirements. Products are already developed, and the compensation plan is designed by the company. The fact that you do not have to worry about managing a large staff complement and cumbersome administrative procedures such as payroll and industrial relations, makes this business model easy to run from the comfort of your home. The fact that this business can be run part-time or full-time is also extremely attractive to women.

Chapter 12

Top Earners Globally

"Network marketing has created more millionaires than any other industry in the history of the world."
—Les Brown

Network marketing has produced millions of high earners across the world. This business model is endorsed by astute investors such as Warren Buffett. Bershire Hathaway, Warren Buffett's investment company, owns three of the most successful network marketing companies in the world. We also know that people like Jim Rohn, Eric Worre, Matt Morris.... all made their fortunes through network marketing.

According to the Top 100 earners in network marketing worldwide (updated list-2020), here is the list of the top 25 global network marketing earners in 2020:

Rank	Name	Organisation	Country	Annual Income (est.)
1	Igor Alberts & Andreea Cimbala	DagCoin - Success Factory	Netherlands & Italy	$26,400,000
2	Jenna Zwagil	MyDailyChoice	USA	$12,720,000

Rank	Name	Organisation	Country	Annual Income (est.)
3	Trin & Jirawan Vichaidith	Nu Skin	Thailand	$11,280,000
4	Rolf Kipp	Forever Living	Germany	$10,800,000
5	Ivan & Monika Tapia	IM Mastery Academy	USA	$10,320,000
6	David Imonitie	IM Mastery Academy	USA	$7,800,000
7	Marco Leonardo Oreggia	Lyconet	Austria	$7,440,000
8	Yager Group (Dexter Yager)	Amway	USA	$7,200,000
9	Jason Brown & Matthew Rosa	IM Mastery Academy	USA	$7,200,000
10	Kristen & Travis Butler	MyDailyChoice	USA	$6,444,000
11	John Haremza	Valentus	USA	$6,000,000
12	Khalid Shaath	Dubli Network – Ominto	UAE	$5,760,000
13	Iulian Cimbala	DagCoin – Success Factory	Japan	$5,580,000
14	Stefania Lo Gatto & Danien Feier	Jeunesse	UAE	$5,520,000
15	Andreas Matuska	Lyconet	Monaco	$5,412,000
16	Mark & Judy Willodson	Elepreneurs	USA	$5,412,000
17	Kim Hui	Jeunesse	China	$5,400,000
18	Jeff Roberti	Juice Plus+	USA	$5,400,000
19	Calvin & Shannon Becerra	Jeunesse	USA	$5,400,000

Rank	Name	Organisation	Country	Annual Income (est.)
20	Amber & Dean De Grasse	New U Life	Canada	$4,860,000
21	Brian McClure	Ambit Energy	USA	$4,800,000
22	Roald Mailly & Patricia Numan	DagCoin – Success Factory	Netherlands	$4,740,000
23	Mario Vielmas	DagCoin – Success Factory	Mexico	$4,200,000
24	Terje Dusend	Lyconet	Norway	$4,200,000
25	Hamza Majdi & Mehdi Ben M'louka	Melius	Morocco & Spain	$4,080,000

Chapter 13

What Do the Experts Say About Network Marketing?

"He who takes advice about MLM from those who have not succeeded in MLM is bound to fail. You don't ask medical advice from a plumber, so why get MLM advice from those who haven't been successful?"

—Simon Chan

Network marketing is a rock-solid business model that has helped millions of people to realise their dreams around the world. Network marketing or direct selling is fast becoming the business model of choice for entrepreneurs in the world today. Here in South Africa even well respected and JSE listed companies such as Clientele Life, have established thriving network marketing divisions. Do not allow people who are ignorant about the industry to convince you that this business model does not work. Let's see what world-renowned experts say about this highly profitable business model:

Chris Widener, author and motivational speaker

"In today's economic uncertainty and turmoil, network marketing has become an even more viable option for those who want to be their own boss, earn a substantial full- or part-time income, and find more time freedom to pursue the things they really love in life. Now more than ever, you can take your future into your own hands by starting your own business and earning substantial profits rather than relying on traditional wages determined by someone else."

**Brian Tracey, motivational public speaker
and self-development author**

"The future of network marketing is unlimited. There is no end in sight. It will continue to grow because better people are getting into it... soon, it will be one of the most respected business methods in the world."

"Network marketing is based purely on relationship selling, which is the state of the art in selling today. Small and large companies throughout the world are realising that individuals selling to their friends and associates is the future of sales, because the critical element in buying is trust."

Art Jonak, founder and president of Mastermind Ventures

"Network marketing is no longer on trial. It is a proven and viable profession. A profession that is helping millions of people get ahead financially and moving them closer to their dreams."

Tim Anderson, marketing professional

"Network marketing allows anyone with little investment, to build their own residual income."

Robert Kiyosaki, businessman and best-selling author

"We found that one business model stood out from the rest. This business model creates passive income but requires relatively little cash investment to start up. It has exceptionally low overhead and can be operated on a flexible part-time basis until it generates enough cash flow for the entrepreneur to transition out of his current full-time job. That business model is called network marketing."

"Everyone who wants to be an entrepreneur should look at a network marketing business. Some of the biggest Fortune 500 companies, such as Citi Bank, Avon, Levis and Smith Barney, distribute their products through network marketing or direct sales system."

"By its very nature and design, network marketing is a strikingly fair, democratic, socially responsible system of generating wealth."

Mark Yarmell, author and network marketing professional

"Network marketing is the only industry that allows common people to earn millions with a minimal investment and zero overhead, coupled with total time freedom and the joy of global travel. There are three magic words that worked for all of us who have made it to the pinnacle, and they will work for you: 'Just don't quit.'"

Kevin Harrington, entrepreneur and business executive

"Without a doubt the most explosive way to be an entrepreneur is in network marketing. You do not need a lot of capital. When you start a business, it costs hundreds of thousands of dollars. In network marketing literally for hundreds of dollars or less you can start a business and the upside is endless."

Tony Robbins, life and business strategist

"What's beautiful about network marketing is that you get all the benefits of being a business owner but you don't have to be worried about supply chain, you don't have to be worried about accounting, especially in the world we're living in today, with technology you can know what's happening in real time, the companies have already set up the software, so it's really picking the right company. And there are a lot of great companies in that area. And it is really realising that you are a value creator. If you can go out and add value to other people's lives, if you can just introduce people to a product or a service that truly is extraordinary. Some products and services cannot just be thrown up on Amazon. They need the story to be told. And if you've found a product or service of that nature and you've found a company that has a generous schedule for being able to reward you, and then you begin to get leverage where it's not just you, where you multiply your efforts through other people, then you get all the benefits of being a business owner without all the headaches and without all the same level of risk! I think network marketing is amazing."

Stephen R. Covey, best-selling author of
The 7 Habits of Highly Effective People

"Network marketing has come of age. It's undeniable that it has become a way to entrepreneurship and independence for millions of people."

Richard Brooke, network marketing executive
and personal development expert

"In network marketing, the people who attract, train and motivate the most salespeople, earn the most money."

Bob Burg, author, speaker and MLM coach

"The successful networkers I know, the ones receiving tons of referrals and feeling truly happy about themselves, continually put the other person's needs ahead of their own."

Mike Dillard, network marketing pro

"Success in this industry is not in finding the right person, but in becoming the right person."

Zig Ziglar & John Hayes, authors of books on network marketing

"Network marketing is a dynamic, exciting, and rapidly expanding profession worldwide. It's also a legitimate profession (though some will try to convince you otherwise) that generates wealth for millions of individuals and contributes positively to our global society."

Unknown

"Understand that network marketing is an ongoing process, not a discrete event. Success comes from making new contacts, following up and keeping in touch."

Keith Ferrazzi, author and entrepreneur

"The currency of real networking is not greed but generosity."

Chinese Proverb

"If you want 1 year of prosperity, grow grain. If you want 10 years of prosperity, grow trees. If you want 100 of prosperity, grow people."

Paul Zane Pilzer, economist and author of books on network marketing

"You only win when you help others win."

Michael S. Clouse, author and lifestyle entrepreneur

"In network marketing, duplication is what success looks like."

Chapter 14

Conclusion

Network marketing gives everyone an equal opportunity to realise their entrepreneurial ambitions. This is the industry where people can start up a big business with little or no capital outlay. In network marketing you are expected to invest time more than money. Time is a commodity that is equally available to all people. As demonstrated in the testimonials above, network marketing is capable of liberating people from all walks of life and of empowering them to achieve financial freedom. This industry has helped millions of people to get ahead in life. Network marketing entrepreneurs can create extra incomes and generate wealth. Robert Kiyosaki in his book *The Business of the 21st Century* puts it this way: "By its very nature and design, network marketing is a strikingly fair, democratic, socially responsible system of generating wealth." This is how I have experienced network marketing in my own wealth-generation journey.

The advantages of network marketing create a clear business case for this industry over traditional business models for the following reasons:

- Flexibility. You can do this business part-time or full-time.

- Low cost of entry.

- Low management control. In this business model you do not have to worry about management of employees or inventory management, etc.

- No billing or accounts receivable.

- There is no discrimination between men, women, or race.

- Quick profitability.

- Leveraged income. In this industry you earn from your own effort and from the efforts of the team that you build and lead.

- The compensation plan is based on performance and nothing else.

- This is a low-risk business model.

- In network marketing you enjoy residual income.

- No commuting.

- Network marketing allows you the opportunity to help others on a massive scale.

The main factors that determine success in network marketing are self-development and dedication. This is not a get-rich-quick scheme. People who are prepared to work hard enjoy great rewards from this industry. The selection of a legitimate network marketing company to partner with is also especially important.

References

AZQuotes. (n.d.). *Top 25 Network Marketing Quotes*. Retrieved from: https://www.azquotes.com/quotes/topics/network-marketing.html

Collins, J. (2001). *Good to Great: Why some companies make the leap ... and others don't*. London: Random House Business Books.

Goodreads. (2021). Network Marketing Quotes. Retrieved from: www.goodreads.com

Kiyosaki, R. & Lechter, S. (1997). Rich Dad Poor Dad. Scottsdale, AZ: Plata Publishing.

Kiyosaki, R.T., Fleming, J. & Kiyosaki, K. (2010). *The Business of the 21st Century*. Lake Dallas, TX: DreamBuilders.

Wood, D.T.S. & Reigner, J. (2020). *Expert reveals the truth about Network Marketing*. Retrieved from: https://www.youtube.com/watch?v=eV9EKF-IBQE

Worre, E. (2013). *Go Pro: 7 steps To Becoming A Network Marketing Professional*. Wichita: Network Marketing Pro Inc.

YouTube.(2017).*DirectSellingMastermindEvents.*Retrievedfrom:https://www.youtube.com/channel/UCtKSkqYCq6gFy5ScyEY0RtA

Index